AQA Primary Assessment
Assessing Writing
Teacher's Handbook

Janet Mort

Text © Janet Mort 2008
Original illustrations © Nelson Thornes Ltd 2008

The right of Janet Mort to be identified as author of this work has been asserted by her in accordance with the Copyright, Designs and Patents Act 1988.

All rights reserved. No part of this publication may be reproduced or transmitted in any form or by any means, electronic or mechanical, including photocopy, recording or any information storage and retrieval system, without permission in writing from the publisher or under licence from the Copyright Licensing Agency Limited, of Saffron House, 6-10 Kirby Street, London EC1N 8TS.

Any person who commits any unauthorised act in relation to this publication may be liable to criminal prosecution and civil claims for damages.

Published in 2008 by:
Nelson Thornes Ltd
Delta Place
27 Bath Road
CHELTENHAM
GL53 7TH
United Kingdom

08 09 10 11 12 / 10 9 8 7 6 5 4 3 2 1

A catalogue record for this book is available from the British Library

978-0-7487-9995-4

Illustrations by Paul Gamble
Cover photograph courtesy of BananaStock Ltd
Page make-up by Fakenham Photosetting Ltd
Printed in Croatia by Zrinski

Acknowledgements
The author and publisher would also like to thank the following for permission to reproduce material:
Qualifications and Curriculum Authority (QCA Enterprises Ltd)

Photographs:
© BananaStock Ltd, except p8 © sats-past-papers.co.uk

The author would like to thank: Glebe Junior School, Derbyshire, especially Nick Raynor (head teacher) and Freda Wilson (Key Stage 2 and assessment leader) and Tickhill St Mary's CE Primary and Nursery School, especially Jayne Boaler (head teacher) and Kate Druce KS2 (Key Stage 2 and assessment leader).

Bibliography
The National Literacy Strategy: Grammar for writing, DfEE, 2000

Primary National Strategy: Primary framework for literacy and mathematics, DFES, 2006

Doncaster Local Authority Primary Literacy Team, *Levelled criteria for the assessment of writing*, 2006

Janet Mort, *Games to get them going*, AQA, 2007

Ros Wilson, *Strategies for immediate impact on writing standards*, Andrell Ltd, 2004

Contents

What do we mean by assessment? 4
Types of assessment
How does assessment help pupils?
How does assessment help teachers?
How will this book help?

Understanding how assessment works 8
Formal, external assessment
Continuous assessment
What do we mean by AfL?

Assessment of writing in practice 11
How children develop as writers
Progression in the Primary National Strategy framework for teaching literacy
Recognising a pupil's performance at each level
Moving pupils from level to level
How to create improvement targets for individual pupils

Using assessment to help pupils learn 31
Assessing writing when marking a pupil's work

Writing clinics 34
Writing clinic 1 – Vocabulary
Writing clinic 2 – Organisation
Writing clinic 3 – Clauses and connectives
Writing clinic 4 – Sentence openers
Writing clinic 5 – Punctuation
Writing clinic 6 – Different text types

Peer and self assessment 52
Responding to success criteria
Using the Photocopy Masters to analyse and assess writing

Preparing for SATs 70
SATs preparation Photocopy Masters
Overview of writing tasks from past test papers

SpikoSpeedoShoes – A board game cover

Assessment is the process by which we as teachers – and our children as learners – make judgements on our pupils' work in order to gauge progress. It enables learners to understand and feel confident about what they can do, and highlights the skills they need to consolidate and develop in order to make progress. Accurate and systematic assessment not only heightens learners' awareness of their strengths and weaknesses, but also informs our lesson planning. In addition, the formal grading or 'levelling' of written outcomes guides us in structuring our teaching groups and in determining the nature and levels of support children require.

What do we mean by *assessment?*

The form of assessment with which parents are probably most familiar are the **End of Key Stage Assessments** (**EKSAs**, commonly known as SATs). Much has been said and written about the extent to which SATs effectively 'measure' the quality of schools (and 'rank' them), and the extent to which they are valuable in genuinely raising educational standards.

Alternative ways of assessing pupils' progress are currently being trialled and introduced. The most significant of these are the **Single Level Tests**, external tests closely linked to teacher assessment. Using evidence gathered in the classroom, teachers make judgements about a pupil's writing level using the criteria on the **Assessing Pupil Progress** (**APP**) guidelines. Teachers then enter pupils for that particular writing level at one of two points in the academic year. External marking of the paper either confirms teacher judgements, or results in the pupil not being awarded the level for which they have been entered.

Although these alternatives for Key Stage 2 assessment are in their early stages, the implications for us as classroom teachers are clear.

Increasingly, the focus is on assessment as part of day-to-day work. Teachers will become much more familiar with **Assessment Focuses** in literacy and will use them in a more focused way to make judgements on a pupil's reading and writing. Teachers will also have a better understanding of a pupil's individual profile in writing.

Finally, the use of externally marked tests to support an individual teacher's judgement means that these judgements can be validated. For many, APP and the Single Level Tests combine both formative and summative assessments in a way that helps teachers and enables pupils to make better progress.

Concern is often expressed that many teachers adopt a superficial, short-term approach to the SATs and 'teach to the test'. Learning in English is achieved in the long term not the short term. It involves revisiting work already covered again and again. If we do not consolidate 'progress' achieved by 'hot-housing' methods, we often find that pupils cannot apply what they have learned in different contexts. Development in English is not necessarily linear. Children may demonstrate unexpected skills despite not having fully grasped apparently easier aspects of work; assessment helps the teacher to recognise such anomalies.

What do we mean by *assessment?*

Most importantly, we should be careful not to reduce assessment in English to a set of hierarchical skills. Language use is creative, and there would be very little great literature if writing could be produced to a formula. Experimentation should always be encouraged as this enables children to explore boundaries and consolidate their understanding. For instance, writers occasionally break some of the generally accepted rules of punctuation for effect. Assessment needs to take this into account and as a result will reward us with a much better picture of a pupil's strengths, progress and potential.

Research indicates that pupils are better motivated to learn, and make faster progress, when they are actively involved in the assessment process. It has become part of good classroom practice to share learning objectives with pupils – to shift the emphasis from teacher to learner – so that pupils can better understand what they are learning, why they are learning it, and how activities might develop their skills. The more reflective pupils become, the more responsible for their learning they are likely to feel, and the keener they will be to improve. The **Assessment for Learning** (**AfL**) strategy now embedded in school practice represents a welcome shift towards pupil-centred learning.

Types of assessment

There are four main types of assessment:

- **Formative assessment** is the process by which a teacher observes, evaluates, discusses or marks a piece of work and identifies specific strengths and weaknesses in a pupil's work to provide a focus for teacher/pupil discussion and pupil self analysis/reflection.

- **Diagnostic assessment** results from formative assessment; i.e. we use the feedback to determine the pupil's needs and how they must plan to meet these needs. Diagnostic assessment might also take the form of tests specifically developed to measure a pupil's particular difficulties.

- **Summative assessment** is the feedback given to a pupil at the end of a marked piece of work. It highlights strengths and weaknesses to be addressed. The term can also be used to describe more formal end-of-unit or end-of-phase tests.

- **Assessment for Learning**, which might be seen as 'day-to-day' assessment, is a process concerned not just with outcomes, but with promoting the whole learning process. By establishing a classroom climate in which both teachers and learners are actively engaged in this process, assessment has more impact and value.

Whilst diagnostic assessment, by its very nature, will be objective, both formative and summative assessment are likely to be selective and partial, targeted to the levels of ability of and perceived priorities for the pupils concerned.

> **Assessment for Learning is the process of seeking and interpreting evidence for use by learners and their teachers to decide where learners are in their learning, where they need to go and how best to get there.**
>
> **Assessment Reform Group, 2002**

Just praising a pupil's work has no formative or diagnostic value; equally, correction of every error is likely to undermine a pupil's self-esteem and prevent them from seeing clearly their priorities in terms of targets to work on.

Summative assessment can become formative in the sense that a folder of work gathered over a period of time might reinforce the need to revisit skills not consolidated during that time. It is worth repeating that things taught in a skills- rather than content-based subject such as English, are not necessarily learned fully in the short term.

How does assessment help pupils?

Assessment helps pupils improve **skills** by:

- providing them with a **context** and **purpose** for their current learning

- **reinforcing their knowledge/understanding of content and skills** (though pupils appreciate praise, surveys of upper Key Stage 2 pupils of different abilities have shown that the most important aspect of teacher feedback is the identification of what they need to improve and advice about how to do so)

- enabling them to **reflect** on their learning in order to utilise it in other contexts

- helping them to **modify their approach** to learning where appropriate

- **relaxing pressure**. It provides 'time out' from 'doing'; reflection time also helps pupils to consider modifications 'on the spot' rather than allow time to lapse.

Assessment can **motivate** pupils by:

- heightening their **awareness of progress** made and providing encouragement whilst recognising targets for improvement

- offering them a **'teaching' role** via peer assessment. It has been suggested that we remember 20% of what we are told but 70% of what we explain to others or work out for ourselves.

In addition, by making teaching/learning criteria transparent, assessment can inform parents and encourage a supportive dialogue between them and their children.

How does assessment help teachers?

Assessment **empowers** teachers by:

- helping them to **understand learners** as individuals and to recognise and understand individual/group/class strengths and weaknesses

- **monitoring rates of progress** and raising awareness of difficulties in assimilation which can help 'pinpoint' areas where support and consolidation are needed

- creating a **structured agenda for feedback** dialogues

- **informing detailed planning**.

Whilst emphasising the value of assessment in providing detailed information about skills development, a caveat is needed. A teacher's advice or suggested improvements can be counter-productive, especially when pupils are experimenting or responding in an original way. Sometimes learners need to be 'given their heads' to pursue their own creative approach or to exercise independent thinking. An informed personal response to reading might be more valuable than a teacher's idea of the 'right answer'. A child who is naturally able to structure ideas might be able to dispense with some stages of the planning of writing. When assessing writing in particular, teachers need to understand that English is primarily about communication and the creative use of language. It is not just a set of discrete skills.

Assessment should also help teachers to appreciate individuality and to recognise that strengths and weaknesses are counter-balanced in a 'best fit' assessment.

What do we mean by *assessment*?

Assessment **supports** teachers by:

- creating a detailed profile of development which helps teachers new to the class to plan using prior knowledge

- ensuring that the new teachers have high (but realistic) expectations of pupils before the 'summer drop' which often necessitates reinforcement of skills previously 'learned' (learning in English being recursive, as previously stated).

How will this book help?

Many teachers find it difficult to assess a pupil's strengths and weaknesses in writing. This book will:

- give an overview of different forms of assessment and the way each helps pupils and teachers in the Key Stage 2 classroom

- provide a level-by-level description of pupils' attainment in each writing Assessment Focus

- identify specific skills to improve a pupil's writing and provide simple progress targets

- provide practical ideas for teaching aspects of sentence structure and punctuation, composition, planning and organisation

- provide self and peer assessment activities for pupils

- suggest how past test papers can be used to help prepare pupils for tests.

In this section we look more closely at each of the main forms of assessment in terms of implications for schools and classroom practice.

Understanding how *assessment* works

Formal, external assessment

Assessing Pupil Progress (APP)

Currently being developed and piloted, APP supports teachers in assessing a pupil's progress in writing through an ongoing review of their work in class. Using a relatively small number of assessment guidelines rather than long lists of assessment criteria or test marks, teachers periodically review evidence of a pupil's written work which they draw from as broad a curriculum as possible. This gives them a profile of an individual pupil's particular strengths and weaknesses. When required, teachers can convert their assessments to National Curriculum levels by following a short step-by-step procedure.

Not only does APP help teachers become more familiar with Assessment Focuses, it also encourages them to consider a range of evidence rather than one piece, to take into account how much support and direct teaching a pupil has received, and to offer pupils more choice of writing tasks.

Although the APP process is not in itself an external assessment, it can be used to determine which externally marked Single Level Test pupils should be entered for (see page 4).

End of Key Stage Assessments (EKSAs)

In May each year, when Year 6 pupils sit EKSAs, commonly referred to as SATs, they are awarded a writing level within the range of Levels 3-5.

The test tasks currently include a Shorter Task (20 minutes including planning time) and a Longer Task (45 minutes including planning time). No choice is given but each task comprises a different text type and has a different purpose. The assessment is therefore as broadly based as possible within the constraints of a test situation. Handwriting is assessed through the Longer Task and spelling through a separate spelling test. Each element has its own mark scheme and marking criteria.

A pupil's individual levels/marks can be analysed and compared to previous years' figures to identify areas of strength or weakness in a school's teaching of writing in the following ways:

- Percentage of boys/girls at each level
- Average writing mark for boys/girls
- Average number of correct spellings for boys/girls
- Percentage of children scoring 50% or over on spelling
- Average handwriting/sentence structure/text structure/composition and effect marks for boys/girls
- Analysis of range of vocabulary used.

In addition, noticeable strengths and weaknesses in a pupil's responses to the tasks set, in punctuation, paragraphing, openings and endings, can be judged from a representative sample of scripts.

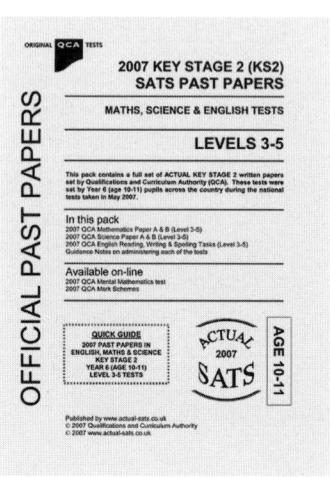

Continuous assessment

Assessment for Learning (AfL)

Assessment for Learning is used increasingly in classrooms both for day-to-day assessments in reading, and also as a way of involving pupils in their own learning.

What do we mean by AfL?

> "Assessment for Learning is any assessment activity that informs the next steps to learning. Assessment for Learning depends crucially on using the information gained."
>
> www.standards.dfes.gov.uk/primaryframeworks/literacy/assessment

Before the AfL approach can become part and parcel of our everyday classroom practice, we need to understand some basic principles.

Assessment for Learning is a form of **continuous assessment** which:

- can be used in a **variety of learning contexts**
- is an **integral** rather than a separate part of lessons
- can be used at **any appropriate point** in the learning process
- focuses on the **process of learning** rather than the end result
- provides learners with useful feedback in a form which helps them recognise what they have already achieved, what they need to do to improve further and how they can achieve this improvement.

Assessment for Learning enables teachers and pupils to work together in an **assessment partnership** which:

- involves pupils by sharing **what**, **why** and **how** they are learning
- enables pupils to become more reflective and independent learners through **self** and **peer assessment**
- helps both teachers and pupils to **check current understanding and progress** and **make informed judgements** about what to do next.

Understanding how assessment works

Changing the assessment climate in YOUR classroom

If AfL is to be effective in promoting learning and raising standards, teachers need to change both ethos and classroom practice.

The classroom where AfL is not used	The AfL classroom
Ethos	
Teachers see themselves as responsible for what and how pupils learn	Pupils are involved in their own learning and are, as a result, more motivated
Teachers emphasise weaknesses to be addressed	The emphasis is on progress, achievement and constructive advice
Pupils see content as being most important	Pupils think about the whole learning process: content, skills and understanding
During the lesson	
Teacher delivers lessons without sharing purpose, process and expectations	Teacher shares purpose, process and expectations of the lesson with pupils
Teacher is the one who knows what the pupils need to do to succeed	Pupils and teachers share a clear understanding of success criteria
Teacher uses very few exemplification materials	Teacher uses clear examples so that pupils understand what they are trying to achieve
Teachers give pupils little time to *think* about their learning	Teachers build in opportunities for pupils to think about and discuss their learning
Pupils rarely review work	Pupils are prepared to improve work after reflection and discussion
Teacher identifies strengths and weaknesses in pupils' work	Pupils share responsibility for evaluating learning outcomes
After the lesson	
Marking of work is superficial, gives only general praise or uses grades/marks	Marking is constructive and helps pupils understand how they can improve
Pupils read teachers' written feedback but do not act on it	Pupils use written feedback to improve work
Pupils move quickly to the next lesson	Previous learning is recalled and links with present learning are established. Time to revisit and improve work is given
Teachers use tests to take snapshots of a pupil's progress	Ongoing use of evidence to help pupils decide where they are now and what they need to do next
Periodic end-of-unit tests provide main source of assessment data	Day-to-day assessment strategies are used by teachers and pupils

In this section we look at how we might use assessment evidence to help pupils improve writing. Firstly, we look at each writing level in turn to give a picture of the whole writer at each National Curriculum level and across all Assessment Focuses. Next we consider common difficulties which we as teachers have when making judgements about a pupil's writing. Finally, improvements are set out in a hierarchy, whenever appropriate, in the form of a pupil's progress targets.

Assessment of writing in *practice*

How children develop as writers

A child's development in writing, best seen as a spiral, is recursive rather than linear. This means that content, language and structure become increasingly sophisticated as writers are exposed to personal and educational experience. Progress may be more uneven than in reading. Some aspects of technical accuracy may be more developed, or lag behind, a child's style or range of vocabulary.

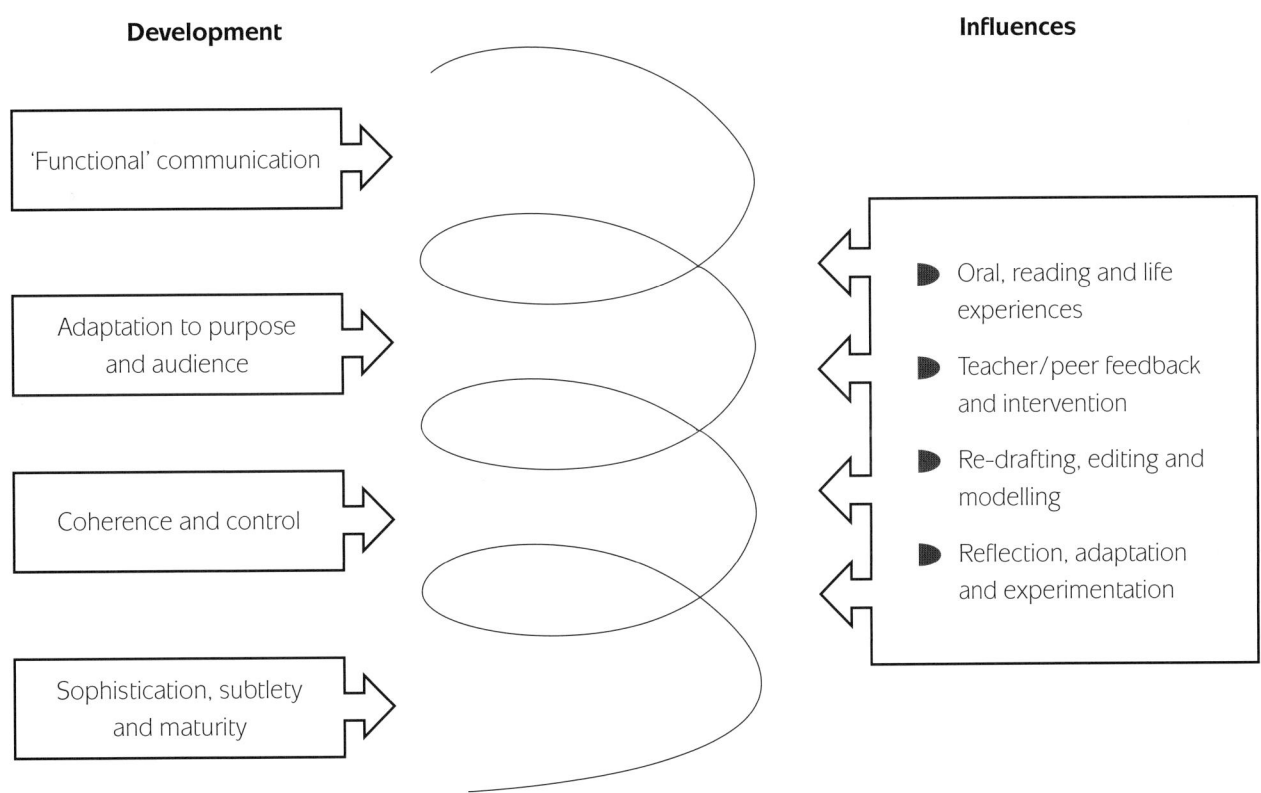

Progression in the Primary National Strategy framework for teaching literacy

Some Assessment Focuses, e.g. AFs 5, 6 and 8, lend themselves more readily to direct teaching. Others depend more on the provision of appropriate opportunities for developing writing experience.

In the Literacy Framework, progression in writing is not shown in terms of progress through Assessment Focuses. Instead, Strands 6, 9, 10, 11 and 12 identify 'a clear set of outcomes for learning progression' in each year.

Strand 6 ('Word structure and spelling') covers Assessment Focus 8.

Strand 9 covers Assessment Focuses 1, 2 and 7 under the heading 'Creating and shaping texts'.

Strand 10 covers Assessment Focuses 3, 4 and 7 under the heading 'Text structure and organisation'.

Strand 11 includes Assessment Focuses 5 and 6 within a set of learning objectives which emphasise variety, clarity and accuracy in the use of sentence structure and punctuation.

Strand 12 ('Presentation') sets out objectives for developing a clear and fluent handwriting style and for using ICT tools to compose and present work.

The progression identified within the Literacy Framework is broadly in line with National Curriculum levels. These are set out in much greater detail in the pages that follow.

Recognising a pupil's performance at each level

The following pages (pages 13-16) give a broad outline of a pupil's performance in writing at each level. Of course, a pupil may well display characteristics of more than one level in any single piece of work. The guidance on pages 17 to 18 then shows how you can help pupils to move up from level to level within each writing Assessment Focus.

Using progress targets to move pupils from level to level

The simple targets presented on Photocopy Masters (PCMs) 1, 2 and 3 (see pages 19-28) concentrate on key areas of writing. They are not intended to cover each level comprehensively, but to provide teachers and pupils with the practical guidance to make progress from level to level. These simple statements can be photocopied for use by pupils on 'improvement target' cards as short- and long-term targets to be kept in writing books or trays. Alternatively, they can be used by teachers as 'success criteria' in individual lessons or with particular pieces of writing. Pupils can also use the statements when making suggestions to improve their own and others' writing.

The table below shows which PCM contains the progress targets for each of the main writing Assessment Focuses. Assessment Focuses 7, 8 and 9 are not included because vocabulary is covered in the statements for the other Assessment Focuses. Spelling is covered by a range of other material (e.g. pages 77-79 in this book).

Assessment Focus	PCM	Pages
AF1 (*write imaginative, interesting and thoughtful texts*) AF2 (*produce texts which are appropriate to task, reader and purpose*)	1a-d	19-22
AF3 (*organise and present whole texts effectively, sequencing and structuring information, ideas and events*) AF4 (*construct paragraphs and use cohesion within and between paragraphs*)	2a-e	23-26
AF5 (*vary sentences for clarity, purpose and effect*) AF6 (*write with technical accuracy of syntax and punctuation in phrases, clauses and sentences*)	3a-d	27-28

A LEVEL 2 writer ...

AF1
(writes imaginative, interesting and thoughtful texts)
- includes some detail to interest the reader, e.g. colour, size, place, simple feelings
- chooses appropriate vocabulary relevant to task
- uses simple adjectives and adverbs, e.g. pretty, slowly.

AF2
(produces texts which are appropriate to task, reader and purpose)
- uses some key features of familiar texts including non-narrative text types, e.g. numbers for instructions, simple headings, playscript conventions
- links writing to task and audience by attempting an appropriate style, e.g. imperatives in instructions
- shows knowledge of story elements in own narratives, e.g. good character facing a difficulty
- shows limited coverage of aspects of the task
- uses simple planning formats
- attempts to meet simple success criteria.

AF3
(organises and presents whole texts effectively, sequencing and structuring information, ideas and events)
- organises familiar text types appropriately
- is aware of how to begin/end some text types
- links ideas using time connectives, e.g. next, then, after.

AF4
(constructs paragraphs and uses cohesion within and between paragraphs)
- sometimes groups ideas into sections
- uses simple cross-references, e.g. 'it' for 'the house'.

AF5
(varies sentences for clarity, purpose and effect)
- uses simple connectives to make compound sentences, e.g. and, but, so
- uses simple connectives to introduce subordinate clauses, e.g. because, if
- uses adjectives, adverbs and prepositions to add detail, e.g. in the corner of the room.

AF6
(writes with technical accuracy of syntax and punctuation in phrases, clauses and sentences)
- begins to understand what a sentence is and sometimes uses full stops and capitals
- sometimes demarcates sentences in other ways, e.g. **?** and **!**
- uses past and present tenses with some accuracy.

AF7
(selects appropriate and effective vocabulary)
- uses vocabulary which is relevant to the task and, sometimes, its purpose
- uses a limited range of interesting vocabulary.

AF8
(uses correct spelling)
- frequently uses phonic strategies to spell unfamiliar words
- spells common monosyllabic words correctly
- knows some spelling patterns, prefixes and suffixes.

Handwriting and presentation
- generally forms letters correctly but overall, size, spacing and position of individual words and letters may be irregular
- joins some letters correctly
- uses the word processor for writing and changing texts; makes choices about fonts, colours and lay-out
- makes choices about how to combine words, pictures and sounds in texts on screen/paper.

A LEVEL 3 writer ...

AF1
(writes imaginative, interesting and thoughtful texts)
- plans to write texts which include interesting details and vocabulary
- moves from one idea or section to the next to give the writing 'pace'
- can compare two different models and use similar techniques, e.g. story openings
- uses adverbial phrases of time and place to add detail, e.g. at the back of the castle, a few moments later.

AF2
(produces texts which are appropriate to task, reader and purpose)
- uses a range of forms, incorporating some features of different text types
- covers main aspects of a writing task but coverage is inconsistent, e.g. writes more in some sections and less in others
- shows awareness of self as a 'writer', e.g. personal statements
- shows awareness of a reader choosing words for a particular effect
- begins to vary style for specific purposes, e.g. to persuade or inform
- uses a wider range of planning formats, e.g. mind maps, story 'mountains'
- evaluates own and other's writing against simple success criteria
- sets simple personal targets with support.

AF3
(organises and presents whole texts effectively, sequencing and structuring information, ideas and events)
- uses paragraphs but not consistently
- takes an overview of the whole piece of writing and groups ideas into sections, not necessarily ordered logically or developed evenly
- includes an opening (often stronger) and an ending (often weaker)
- links some paragraphs/sections, e.g. as well as, the following day, I also think
- uses headings and other divisions to separate sections.

AF4
(constructs paragraphs and uses cohesion within and between paragraphs)
- groups ideas into sections but not always in a logical sequence
- begins to use opening sentences to indicate what the section is about
- uses pronouns and nouns to refer to the same thing, e.g. dog, it, Benjie, he, her pet.

AF5
(varies sentences for clarity, purpose and effect)
- uses simple compound and complex sentences
- uses a range of common connectives to introduce subordinate clauses, e.g. when, after, before
- begins to alter the order of main and subordinate clause for variety
- experiments with varied ways of opening sentences, e.g. adverbs
- uses adverbial phrases of time and place to add detail, e.g. a few days later, in the playground
- attempts to use a range of punctuation, e.g. apostrophes.

AF6
(writes with technical accuracy of syntax and punctuation in phrases, clauses and sentences)
- uses a range of punctuation to demarcate sentences, e.g. . ! and ?
- uses 1st/3rd person consistently
- uses a range of tenses accurately
- uses speech marks in dialogue
- uses commas in lists correctly and sometimes for other purposes, often incorrectly
- shows accurate subject/verb agreement most of the time
- re-reads and checks sentences for missing words.

AF7
(selects appropriate and effective vocabulary)
- uses text-specific and own choices of interesting vocabulary
- uses familiar and 'taught' genre and task-specific vocabulary, e.g. words given by teacher as part of the task or genre
- chooses simple words for effect, e.g. spooky, terrifying
- uses a limited range of noun phrases, e.g. the huge brown gate; adjectives, e.g. tasty; and adverbial phrases, e.g. next to the fence.

Handwriting and presentation
- shows more consistency in the spacing, size and orientation of letters and words
- uses joins, e.g. a, o, p, g, t, but not consistently
- makes choices for effect, e.g. block capitals
- on paper and on screen, links the choice of format to the purpose of the writing or to create a specific effect.

AF8
(uses correct spelling)
- uses existing knowledge of simple spelling patterns, prefixes and suffixes to attempt unfamiliar words
- learns and applies some spelling rules, e.g. double consonants.

A LEVEL 4 writer ...

AF1
(writes imaginative, interesting and thoughtful texts)
- writes imaginatively using detail and well-chosen vocabulary to engage the reader, e.g. by creating suspense or humour
- experiments in writing transformations, changing text type and purpose, e.g. writing a narrative as a diary, using information texts to write a persuasive letter
- uses some figurative language effectively
- maintains the pace to keep the reader interested.

AF2
(produces texts which are appropriate to task, reader and purpose)
- uses a range of forms and the main features of different text types confidently
- shows balanced coverage of points
- adapts writing for a specific purpose and audience
- establishes viewpoint by adopting a consistent stance or tone
- adapts style for more formal purposes with support
- selects from and uses a range of planning formats
- evaluates writing against a range of success criteria and suggests improvements
- understands and sets personal targets.

AF3
(organises and presents whole texts effectively, sequencing and structuring information, ideas and events)
- in main genres, uses a range of features to organise texts appropriately, e.g. letter format, playscript layout
- generally uses linked and sequenced paragraphs
- develops introductions and conclusions in more detail
- maps simple text structures independently, e.g. draws lay-out for a letter showing awareness of the whole text.

AF4
(constructs paragraphs and use cohesion within and between paragraphs)
- uses topic (main) sentence to indicate paragraph content
- orders ideas logically within paragraphs
- sometimes links ideas to each other and to the topic sentence
- uses ongoing references to link ideas, e.g. 'another good thing about ...'
- uses a wider range of different words and phrases when referring to the same thing, e.g. the dog, Benjie, the poor little animal, he
- uses connective phrases, sometimes mechanically, for cohesion, e.g. firstly, secondly, in addition, moreover.

AF5
(varies sentences for clarity, purpose and effect)
- uses simple, compound and complex sentences appropriately for text type, purpose and audience
- uses a range of connectives, e.g. who, which, while, although, whenever
- uses a range of punctuation in different contexts, e.g. commas in lists and to mark clauses
- uses a range of tenses, e.g. past, present, future, conditional
- experiments with the use of a wider range of punctuation, e.g. brackets, colons, hyphens.

AF6
(writes with technical accuracy of syntax and punctuation in phrases, clauses and sentences)
- demarcates sentences accurately using . ! and ?
- uses commas correctly for lists and sometimes to separate clauses
- uses a wide range of punctuation accurately, e.g. speech marks
- re-reads and checks work for omissions and other errors.

Handwriting and presentation
- maintains consistency and control of ascenders, descenders, joins, size, spacing and orientation
- adapts handwriting and presentation on paper/screen for particular purposes and effects, e.g. decorative, italics, underlining, highlighting
- presents texts of all types using a wide range of ICT programmes effectively to communicate information and ideas
- analyses and improves inconsistencies in handwriting.

AF7
(selects appropriate and effective vocabulary)
- uses technical and genre-specific vocabulary independently and appropriately
- uses a range of well-chosen words and phrases, e.g. to create mood
- uses figurative language experimentally.

AF8
(uses correct spelling)
- categorises a wide range of spellings according to structure, patterns and prefixes
- carries out spelling investigations
- checks and corrects own spellings more consistently.

A LEVEL 5 writer ...

AF1
(writes imaginative, interesting and thoughtful texts)

- uses effective detail and selects vocabulary precisely to convey more subtle meaning, e.g. 'aggressive' for 'angry'
- uses a range of techniques to vary pace, e.g. length of sentence, balance between events, descriptions and dialogue
- uses a range of narrative techniques to add interest, e.g. flashbacks, simultaneous events
- may present different viewpoints to engage the reader.

AF2
(produces texts which are appropriate to task, reader and purpose)

- handles a full range of text types with confidence, using all key features
- covers main points extensively and in a balanced fashion
- sustains an awareness of audience and purpose through direct address, comments, questions and appeals
- independently links style and form to match purpose and audience
- can analyse writing models confidently
- sets personal targets and evaluates progress independently
- plans quickly and effectively using a full range of planners.

AF3
(organises and presents whole texts effectively, sequencing and structuring information, ideas and events)

- uses full range of organisational features and layout conventions across a wide range of texts
- links paragraphs effectively to give the whole piece coherent 'shape'
- makes an impact on the reader by using detailed introductions and conclusions for effect
- considers the order of paragraphs and how this might improve the overall effectiveness of the writing.

AF4
(constructs paragraphs and uses cohesion within and between paragraphs)

- deliberately varies the length and structure of selected paragraphs for effect
- selects and develops a specific focus for each paragraph
- introduces and concludes paragraphs to support the chosen focus
- groups and orders sentences to develop the focus
- uses connective words and phrases discriminatingly to order and emphasise points, and to make links between paragraphs
- uses a wide range of alternative vocabulary to create reference chains, e.g. the dog, Benjie, the poor little animal, he, the unfortunate creature, Jane's pet.

AF5
(varies sentences for clarity, purpose and effect)

- uses full range of simple, compound and complex sentences, varying the length, order and structure deliberately for effect
- writes economically for effect, e.g. 'John, a stick-in-the-mud technophobe, ...'
- uses connectives in pairs to order ideas or add detail, e.g. 'not only ... but also ...'.

AF6
(writes with technical accuracy of syntax and punctuation in phrases, clauses and sentences)

- uses a full range of tense and verb forms accurately and appropriately, e.g. passive for more formal purposes, present tense for effect, conditional to suggest possibility
- uses a full range of punctuation confidently and accurately to support meaning and for effect
- checks work and identifies most omissions and errors.

AF7
(selects appropriate and effective vocabulary)

- uses Standard English, colloquialisms and dialect deliberately for purpose and effect
- uses a wide range of apt vocabulary with precision, e.g. descriptive, technical
- shows creativity in the use of figurative language
- uses comparisons, puns and word-patterns appropriately, e.g. 'Time to change? I say no change to the time!'.

AF8
(uses correct spelling)

- spells unfamiliar words by drawing on existing knowledge of a wide range of word roots, derivations, rules and patterns
- applies spelling rules, including anomalies, confidently
- organises and carries out spelling investigations independently and explains observations confidently.

Handwriting and presentation

- writes using a fluent, legible and consistent style which engages the reader
- adapts presentational choices to suit specific purposes and audiences after reviewing initial choices.

Moving pupils from level to level – AFs 1 to 6

AF1

To move pupils from level to level in AF1 (*write imaginative, interesting and thoughtful texts*) teachers need to:

- use pupil's experiences and familiar topics as starting points for writing
- provide a range of stimulating reading material and use these to model writing
- teach pupils how to annotate and analyse models
- give pupils freedom of choice when writing in personal journals
- use unusual stimuli to generate imaginative ideas, e.g. the Gorgon's head
- give opportunities for discussion to help pupils clarify their ideas
- encourage pupils to experiment when changing one text type into another or combining text types
- set clear success criteria against which pupils can carry out peer and self assessment.

AF2

To move pupils from level to level in AF2 (*produce texts which are appropriate to task, reader and purpose*) teachers need to:

- provide models of an increasingly wide range of text types
- provide simplified summaries of each text type for pupils to refer to when writing independently (see pages 49–51)
- teach pupils how to annotate and analyse models
- use a broad curriculum to provide pupils with opportunities for choosing text type, audience and purpose
- set clear success criteria against which pupils can carry out peer and self assessment.

AF3, AF4

To move pupils from level to level in AF3 (*organise and present whole texts effectively, sequencing and structuring information, ideas and events*) and AF4 (*construct paragraphs and use cohesion within and between paragraphs*) teachers need to:

- provide a range of planning formats
- give writing frames to support the teaching of text structure
- provide opportunities for pupils to evaluate different structures
- provide opportunities for pupils to discuss, group and sequence ideas
- teach pupils how to annotate and analyse models
- set clear success criteria against which pupils can carry out peer and self assessment.

AF5, AF6

To move pupils from level to level in AF5 (*vary sentences for clarity, purpose and effect*) and AF6 (*write with technical accuracy of syntax and punctuation in phrases, clauses and sentences*) teachers need to:

- use stimulating models to encourage experimentation with sentence structure
- teach pupils how to annotate and analyse models
- play a variety of oral games to practise using grammar and to consolidate skills (see J. Mort (2007) *Games to get them going*)
- provide pupils with opportunities to check, edit and re-draft work
- set clear personal targets
- set clear success criteria against which pupils can carry out peer and self assessment.

Moving pupils from level to level – AFs 7 and 8, presentation

AF 7

To move pupils from level to level in AF7 (*select appropriate and effective vocabulary*) teachers need to:

- provide interesting reading material to increase a pupil's range of vocabulary
- model the use of a wide range of vocabulary in everyday classroom contexts across the whole curriculum
- provide pupils with opportunities for oral work in a wide range of contexts
- provide opportunities to practice using a thesaurus
- display and use relevant word banks and encourage the use of personal word books
- teach pupils how to annotate and analyse models
- set clear success criteria against which pupils can carry out peer and self assessment.

AF 8

To move children from level to level in AF8 (*use correct spelling*) teachers need to:

- use a variety of teaching strategies, e.g. visual, auditory and kinaesthetic
- focus on spelling through, for example, giving pupils the opportunity to categorise spellings, identify patterns, carry out investigations, apply rules, learn mnemonics, draw calligrams and devise own tests
- give pupils practice at using dictionaries to check for accuracy
- do a range of spelling puzzles (see pages 77-79).

Presentation

To move children from level to level in handwriting and presentation teachers need to:

- provide opportunities to practice and consolidate formation of letters, correct joins, size and orientation
- provide contexts on both screen and paper in which choices about presentation and handwriting can be made
- encourage pupils to evaluate handwriting and presentation choices independently (see pages 52-69).

Name _____   Class _____

PCM 1a – AF1 and AF2 (Level 2)

To improve how I think of and write down my ideas to make my writing more lively and interesting, and to impress readers of my work, I need to:

- [ ] make my ideas 'grow' by adding detail to each one

- [ ] make my ideas, and the words I use to explain them, 'fit' the title

- [ ] add interesting adjectives and adverbs to describe people, things and places, e.g. 'amazing' and 'nastily'

- [ ] give stories clear openings and endings

- [ ] have at least two things happening, one after the other, in stories

- [ ] know about other kinds of writing and what makes them different, e.g. instructions, playscripts, letters

- [ ] use these features in my own writing

- [ ] put down ideas on a planner and follow them when writing

- [ ] try to make my writing match success targets.

Name _____ Class _____

PCM 1b – AF1 and AF2 (Level 3)

- [ ] make my writing more interesting by adding details, explanations and my own comments

- [ ] decide when to move to the next part/event so that my writing is interesting to read

- [ ] describe a setting, one or more characters, and put my events in a sensible order in stories

- [ ] read and think about the work of other writers and 'rob' good ideas

- [ ] use phrases like 'at the back of', 'surrounded by …' and 'a few moments later …' for detail

- [ ] try to cover all parts of the writing as shown on my planners

- [ ] be able to write different kinds of text (e.g. letter, report, play script, explanation) so that they look like models I have read and have some of the same 'ingredients', e.g. headings, addresses, stage directions

- [ ] know why I am writing (e.g. to tell a reader how to do or make something – INSTRUCTIONS; tell a reader all about a topic – REPORT; to let someone know my opinion and get them to share it – PERSUADE; to entertain – STORY, POEM or DESCRIPTION)

- [ ] use different kinds of planners

- [ ] think about my own and others' writing and decide how it could be improved.

Name _____ Class _____

PCM 1c – AF1 and AF2 (Level 4)

To improve how I think of and write down my ideas to make my writing more lively and interesting, and to impress readers of my work, I need to:

- [ ] take one kind of writing and use interesting ways to turn it into another kind
- [ ] use a good range of 'amazing' words and phrases
- [ ] be able to build up an atmosphere to make my reader feel nervous or happy
- [ ] use interesting comparisons to make my writing more lively and detailed
- [ ] keep a reader interested by describing settings and characters in enough detail, by writing good openings and endings, and by moving on to the next event or section
- [ ] be confident that I know the 'ingredients' of many different kinds of writing and how to use them
- [ ] read and think about the work of other writers and pick out a range of different features to discuss, criticise and use
- [ ] be clear about why I am writing and who I am writing for, and make my writing show this
- [ ] be able to present my own and other people's viewpoints
- [ ] use a range of different planners to organise my ideas
- [ ] think about targets for my own and others' writing and how successfully they have been met
- [ ] identify my own simple targets and work towards them.

Name _____   Class _____

PCM 1d AF1 and AF2 (Level 5)

To improve how I think of and write down my ideas to make my writing more lively and interesting, and to impress readers of my work, I need to:

- [ ] be a writer who is not afraid to experiment and try to find unusual ways of approaching a piece of writing
- [ ] have a very wide vocabulary and choose words which exactly fit the purpose or create a particular effect
- [ ] know why I am writing and show this by using the appropriate language, tone and organisation of my ideas
- [ ] know for whom I am writing and show this by using the appropriate language, tone and techniques to appeal to my reader, e.g.
  - formal/informal language
  - direct address
  - questions
  - presentation of arguments for and against with supporting reasons
- [ ] use a range of techniques to make my stories interesting, e.g.
  - flashbacks, flash forwards, simultaneous events
  - shorter and longer sentences and paragraphs for effect
  - some fast-paced sections with events happening quickly
  - mixture of dialogue, events and description
- [ ] be a writer who knows very clearly what type of writing I am composing and which features should be included to make the type easily recognisable, e.g.
  - different types of story (e.g. myth, adventure)
  - diary
  - biography/autobiography
  - recount
  - description of scene/person
  - rules
  - instructions
  - directions
  - explanations
  - non-chronological reports
  - adverts
  - leaflets
  - letters
  - playscripts
  - poems
- [ ] cover all main points or sections of a particular piece of writing in detail
- [ ] plan all aspects of a piece of writing quickly and choose the best type of planner for the job
- [ ] select specific aspects of other writers' work to read, annotate and discuss
- [ ] be able to set my own targets for writing and assess my progress independently.

Name _____ Class _____

PCM 2a – AF3 and AF4

Improving how I group my ideas, how I begin and end my writing and how I put my ideas in order.

Producing a whole piece of writing is a bit like building a house. Just as we would have a design for the whole house, so we need to think about the 'shape' of our whole piece of writing.

First we need 'foundations' (in other words the ideas we are going to put into our writing).

Then, just as we need to decide how many windows we would like in our house and where to put them, so we also need to decide how many paragraphs or sections we need and what order and length they should be.

We must also decide what sort of front door to have (the beginning of our writing) and back door (ending).

Name _____ Class _____

PCM 2a: continued ...

We might also think about adding a conservatory or front porch (other features of particular texts, e.g. letter headings, bullet points, stage directions).

Just as in a house we need to cement bricks together, so when writing paragraphs or sections, we need to 'glue' our ideas together. We do this by:

- using pronouns, e.g. he, it, they
- using connective words and phrases, e.g. on the other hand, finally, later that week.

We can also try to vary the way we describe something, using different words each time it's mentioned, e.g. the dog, the little terrier, Towser.

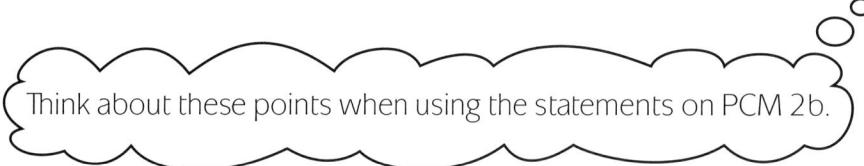

Think about these points when using the statements on PCM 2b.

Name _____ Class _____

PCM 2b – AF3 and AF4 (Level 2)

To improve how I group my ideas, how I begin and end my writing and how I put my ideas in order, I need to:

- ☐ look carefully at a model of the text I am writing and try to do the same
- ☐ make sure that I begin and end my work with a clear opening sentence and a clear closing sentence
- ☐ link these opening and closing sentences to my title
- ☐ put ideas about one thing together in one section
- ☐ use connectives like 'and', 'but', 'so' and 'then' to join sentences together
- ☐ use pronouns, instead of nouns, e.g. I, me, it, they.

--✂---

Name _____ Class _____

PCM 2c – AF3 and AF4 (Level 3)

To improve how I group my ideas, how I begin and end my writing and how I put my ideas in order, I need to:

- ☐ think about what my type of writing needs, e.g. headings, sub-headings
- ☐ include two or more ideas in my opening and ending paragraphs
- ☐ link my opening and ending to each other and to the title
- ☐ group my ideas together in clear sections and try to put sections in the best order
- ☐ try to use paragraphs and remember to show where a new one starts
- ☐ use a main sentence ('coat hanger') at the start of each section to let the reader know what it is going to be about
- ☐ use ordering connectives like 'firstly,' 'next' and 'finally' to join sentences
- ☐ try not to repeat a word, but think of replacements, e.g. 'litter' for 'rubbish'.

Name _____ Class _____

PCM 2d – AF3 and AF4 (Level 4)

To improve how I group my ideas, how I begin and end my writing and how I put my ideas in order, I need to:

- [ ] know what my writing needs to have so that it is organised, e.g. paragraphs, columns, pictures
- [ ] make my first and last paragraphs contain details which introduce or 'sum up' the rest of the writing
- [ ] group my ideas together in clear paragraphs most of the time
- [ ] show clearly where each paragraph begins by starting a new line/indenting
- [ ] choose which order to put my paragraphs in and know why I have made each choice
- [ ] link paragraphs with phrases such as 'as well as' or 'on the other hand'
- [ ] start each paragraph with a main sentence 'coat hanger'
- [ ] use good connective phrases like 'Another good thing about …' and 'In addition …' inside paragraphs
- [ ] think of other good words and phrases so that I do not repeat words unnecessarily.

✂ -

Name _____ Class _____

PCM 2e – AF3 and AF4 (Level 5)

To improve how I group my ideas, how I begin and end my writing and how I put my ideas in order, I need to:

- [ ] include all organisational features for my text
- [ ] make my first and last paragraphs very detailed and include questions for the reader
- [ ] start a new paragraph for a new topic, change of time, place, action or dialogue
- [ ] write about two events happening at the same time in stories
- [ ] sometimes use a flashback or 'jump' forward in time in stories
- [ ] deliberately make some paragraphs short/long, fast/slow for effect
- [ ] put my ideas in order within paragraphs with the most important idea first or last
- [ ] use connective words and phrases sensibly to link paragraphs and ideas within paragraphs
- [ ] use many different words and phrases instead of a noun, e.g. the dog, Bobby, the terrier, the little animal, the poor creature.

Name _____ Class _____

PCM 3a – AF5 and AF6 (Level 2)

To improve how I write sentences and use punctuation, I need to:

- [ ] join sentences together with 'and', 'but' and 'so'
- [ ] begin sentences with 'then' and 'next'
- [ ] use 'because', 'if' and 'when' to add another idea to a sentence
- [ ] include adjectives like 'amazing', and adverbs like 'slowly', when describing
- [ ] recognise sentences, and use capital letters and full stops at beginning and end
- [ ] use ? and ! to show questions and exclamations
- [ ] use past verbs like 'played' and 'was playing' and present verbs like 'plays' and 'is playing' correctly.

Name _____ Class _____

PCM 3b – AF5 and AF6 (Level 3)

To improve how I write sentences and use punctuation, I need to:

- [ ] use different kinds of sentence, e.g. simple, compound, complex
- [ ] use a range of connectives, e.g. before, after, which
- [ ] turn sentences round, e.g.
  'I played out because I was bored.' ➡ 'Because I was bored, I played out.'
- [ ] find different ways to begin sentences, e.g. Amazingly …, Minutes later …, In one corner …
- [ ] add detail to show *when*, *where* and *how*, e.g. after some time …, at the back of the shed …, with a frown …
- [ ] generally use capital letters, full stops, question and exclamation marks accurately
- [ ] use commas for lists
- [ ] try to use commas (for pauses), speech marks, apostrophes and other punctuation
- [ ] use many different verbs accurately
- [ ] re-read and check sentences for missing words and mistakes especially plurals, e.g. the bo**ys** pla**y**, the bo**y** pla**ys**.

Name _____   Class _____

PCM 3c – AF5 and AF6 (Level 4)

To improve how I write sentences and use punctuation, I need to:

- [ ] think about the *type* of writing when using different sentence structures: simple, compound and complex
- [ ] use a range of connectives in different places in sentences, e.g. who, which, whenever, although, while
- [ ] use correct punctuation (capital letters, **,** **.** **!** and **?**, **"** and **"**, **'** and **'**) in all sentences
- [ ] experiment with the use of brackets, hyphens, colons, semi-colons and ellipsis
- [ ] use a range of tenses accurately.

Name _____   Class _____

PCM 3d – AF5 and AF6 (Level 5)

To improve how I write sentences and use punctuation, I need to:

- [ ] think about the *type* of writing, the *reason* for writing and *who* the writing is for when using different sentence structures for effect: simple, compound and complex
- [ ] use connectives in pairs, e.g. 'whenever … then …', 'not only … but also …'
- [ ] use a full range of punctuation accurately
- [ ] use a full range of tenses and verb forms accurately and appropriately.

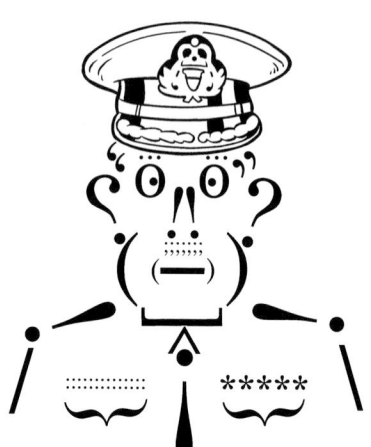

How to create improvement targets for individual pupils

You need to consider the following principles when setting individual improvement targets for pupils in writing.

 Personal profile

In writing generally, and in different types of writing in particular, each pupil will have an individual profile with strengths and weaknesses in different areas. If we are to set improvement targets we need to make them pertinent to each pupil's particular needs. This means that we must have a good grasp of progression in each Assessment Focus. The detailed lists on pages 13-16 will help you to identify where a pupil is now and where they need to be.

 Relevant tasks

Most writing Assessment Focuses are relevant to most writing tasks and text types. However, it would be totally impractical and counter-productive for pupils to focus on more than a few key elements in any one piece of work. Instead, we select Assessment Focuses according to year group, the needs of the class, individual pupils, availability of texts, results from previous assessments, planning and Literacy Framework guidance.

These key elements are taught continuously but we should also look for opportunities to encourage writers to be more independent. We need to know what they can do with less specific teacher guidance and whether they can apply what we have taught them in different tasks and contexts. Opportunities for this are more easily found in cross-curricular work.

 Optimum number

Clearly, the number of improvement targets for each pupil will depend on such things as the pupil's ability, attitude and rate of progress. The nature of the targets set might also determine how many we give pupils at any one time. Generally speaking, pupils should have no more than three, but even then, they can suffer from 'target fatigue', especially when we consider they may also have targets for reading and maths. Make the process manageable.

 Giving a guarantee

When setting an improvement target, make explicit to pupils what they have to do and how/when they need to do it so that progress will be made. The more you believe that success is guaranteed, the more confidence you will inspire and the more easily the target will be met.

 Review

Finding time to review individual improvement targets is difficult, to say the least. Make use of 'buddy' response sheets, improvement target cards or annotations on work to jot down evidence as and when writing is discussed or when marking written evidence in all areas of the curriculum. The more pupils are involved in their own target setting and the more they understand particular targets, the easier it becomes to review progress. Discussion with a writing partner enables pupils to reflect on their own progress. Encourage pupils to carry out neat highlighting in margins to show where evidence can be found.

 Evidence

Evidence in writing (work in progress, completed pieces, teacher, peer and self assessments, planners, oral notes) is easily found. Tasks can be adapted for a particular Assessment Focus (see 'Relevant tasks', above). You might also consider unmarked writing journals in which pupils write for short 15-minute sessions on any topic in whichever way they choose. Reluctant writers in particular find this motivating and liberating, but it is important to establish the following ground rules:

- Writers should not use inappropriate language.
- Nothing bad or untrue about a real person should be included.
- Pupils should be aware that some work (identified by the teacher) will be shared after a session.
- Pupils may show the teacher their work after a session.

Small steps

Break down each improvement target into manageable chunks to show pupils exactly how and what they are going to need to do. Group pupils whenever possible so that they can help each other assess progress.

Example:

> My target is 'to use speech marks in dialogue'.

1 *From a text you are reading, find two examples of dialogue.*
2 *Copy accurately, using a different colour for the speech marks.*
3 *Copy two more examples without speech marks. Put the speech marks in and check against your text. Correct if necessary.*
4 *Discuss with your 'buddy' the rules for using speech marks.*
5 *Complete Exercise X for your teacher to mark. Correct if necessary.*
6 *Use speech marks in your own writing. Discuss and highlight incorrect use of speech marks.*
7 *Continue until you are accurate.*

 Simple

Keep individual improvement targets as simple and practical as possible. Choose KEY targets for each level and stick to these to make the process manageable.

Opportunity for choice of ...	Context
Topic	Pupils prepare a short talk on their Aztec 'specialism', e.g. Tenochtitlan, medicine, astrology, the calendar, warfare. Pupils choose three developments to research/write about in more detail from a history timeline, e.g. the Victorians.
Purpose	*Save the Rainforest!* Pupils choose between writing a letter to a newspaper setting out facts (persuade/inform) and writing a letter home describing their experiences of a trip up the Amazon (entertain/amaze/inform).
Text type	Following a field study trip, pupils choose between writing a recount, an information leaflet describing the centre or a letter of thanks. (Key features of different text types can be given to children as 'bookmarks', PCMs 9–10, see pages 50–51.)
Point of view	Write about the party from Mr Tom's or William's point of view in *Goodnight Mr Tom.*
Level of formality	In a topic on the local environment, pupils want to raise the issue of the number of potholes in the local area. They choose between writing a formal letter to their MP or an informal diary entry describing problems encountered on their way home from school.
Vocabulary	For a piece of writing entitled 'How a teabag works' or a report on the 'Pack-it-in bag', pupils select and use technical vocabulary to suit the task, e.g. malleable, infuse, waterproof, perforated.
Lay-out	Contrasting localities. Pupils choose how to present an account of a child's day, e.g. Venn diagram, paragraphs using a writing frame, diary of key times/events presented in a table.
Organisation of ideas	Choice of planners, e.g. mind map, storyboard or flow chart (see pages 19–28 for more ideas on teaching pupils how to make choices about text structure and organisation).

Using *assessment* to help pupils learn

Assessing writing can be daunting. Don't be afraid to ask for support in checking judgements from colleagues and welcome any opportunity to check your judgements at moderation meetings. You will only develop accurate standards through practice and discussion with other teachers.

Detailed assessment criteria can be difficult to understand, and may even appear unhelpful when applied to a specific genre (e.g. playscript) because they have to cover a wide range of types of writing.

However, there are a few key assessment Strands which relate to all kinds of writing:

- Content
- Vocabulary
- Structure
- Sentence structures
- Punctuation
- Spelling
- Presentation

Assessing writing levels is not an exact science and in some instances, there may be an element of 'trade-off'. Inaccurate spelling can be the most obvious weakness in writing, but an imaginative description using ambitious but incorrectly spelt vocabulary may well be better than one that is technically perfect but written in simple sentences using only simple vocabulary.

The flow chart opposite gives a simplified step-by-step approach to the assessment of a pupil's writing.

Read the assessment criteria carefully and highlight key words.

↓

Read a collection of five pieces and arrange in approximate rank order.

↓

If using a mark scheme take one Strand at a time.

↓

Begin (AF 5 and 6) then (AF 3 and 4) then (AF 1 and 2)
or
Begin (AF 1 and 2) then (AF 3 and 4) then (AF 5 and 6)

↓

Find and consider evidence for each Strand.

- Where is it?
- How much evidence is there?
- Where is the writing stronger and where weaker than the criteria?
- How much support has been given?
- How much of the writing is original?

↓

Make a judgement

↓

Set three targets for the pupil – two short-term and one long-term.

↓

From class assessments, select a strong, average and weak script and ask a colleague for a second opinion.

↓

Discuss targets with pupil and keep a record for both of you to consult/tick in subsequent pieces.

Assessing writing when marking a pupil's work

When marking a pupil's ongoing work, you will be operating within assessment frameworks and applying their criteria, but your approach will be different as you need to give useful feedback to pupils whose writing you are trying to improve. Sometimes it is helpful to give a pupil general feedback on writing progress by marking a number of elements in the whole piece. At other times, you will need to mark solely to success criteria relevant to the specific teaching focus of the lesson.

Summative comments need to be brief but positive in identifying progress, effort and achievements. Targets for improvement need to be clear, brief and realistic, i.e. identifying the next small step. Remember that writing skills are developed over time (like your assessment skills!). The learning is recursive, too – sometimes pupils appear to go backwards in some areas while they are focusing on others.

Sharing mark scheme assessment criteria with pupils helps them to see where they need to improve, though criteria may need to be explained and simplified to make them accessible (see pages 52–60). Peer re-drafting/editing/discussion consolidates awareness of skills levels and self-assessment likewise, e.g. setting targets and 'logging' improvement points.

Occasionally it is useful to ask pupils for their views on the way teachers mark written work. The results of some of the more interesting questions in one such survey are given below. Equal numbers of Year 5 and Year 6 boys and girls (120 in all) completed the questionnaire anonymously.

'MAKING YOUR MARK' QUESTIONNAIRE

This questionnaire is designed to find out what YOU think about the way teachers mark your writing. Your opinions are very important so please give an honest answer!

1   When teachers mark your writing, what is most important to you?

The teacher tells me how I could improve	*72%*
The teacher picks up all of my mistakes	*8%*
I am given examples of improvements	*7%*
The teacher picks up SOME of my mistakes	*5%*
Spelling mistakes are corrected	*5%*
The teacher makes good comments about my writing	*3%*

2   Do you understand the comments that teachers put on your writing?

Please circle: Always *20%*   Mostly *71%*   Partly *9%*   Never *0%*

3   Please circle: Teachers should correct   all   most   some   none   of your incorrect spellings.

All *40%*   Most *45%*   Some *15%*   None *0%*

4   What annoys you about teachers' marking of your writing?

Nothing!   (By far the most popular response. Other quotes are given below.)
It's too messy.
They put too many comments.
When they don't put a level at the end of your work, e.g. 5a, 5b.
They should print their own writing so anyone can understand.
When they put a lot of bad comments so you don't do well next time.
When they put hard [sic] comments which put some children off.
When they use words that you don't understand.
Circling words and letters.
All of the pen all over your work when you have done it neat and tidy [sic].

5   Do adults at home take much notice of the way your writing is marked?

Please circle: Yes *63%*   No *5%*   Sometimes *32%*

6   What sort of things do they say about the marking of your writing?

It shows I could do a lot better.
That sometimes you can't read the writing.
There is too much ink on/that the teacher puts too much.
They sometimes do say something but not always because they believe that teachers know what they are doing.
It is good because they can see all my good and bad writing.
They say it's fairly marked.
They ask me why I don't do what the teacher says.

7   Marking makes me want to improve my writing …

Please circle: Always *42%*   Sometimes *43%*   Not usually *15%*

In this section you will find six Writing Clinics to help pupils improve aspects of writing they often find difficult:
Vocabulary (see below)
Organisation (see page 38)
Clauses and connectives (see page 44)
Sentence openers (see page 46)
Punctuation (see page 48).
Different text types (see page 49)

Writing Clinics

WRITING CLINIC 1
Vocabulary

Assessments of writing often identify a weakness in both the range and the quality of a pupil's vocabulary. This section gives suggestions for a whole-school *Word robbery book*, and for games and activities to develop pupils' vocabulary.

A Word robbery book

Pupils need to use words imaginatively and appropriately for any given task, reader and purpose. This might involve decisions about technical or specialist words, the best descriptive phrases to create atmosphere, formal or informal phrases, genre-specific words and using specific words to vary sentences and to add detail.

Vocabulary acquisition is a long-term process and it goes without saying that all pupils should have access to a range of different thesauruses and know how to use them confidently.

Unfortunately, much of the vocabulary development that teachers do is lost when pupils move from class to class. For example, in Years 2 and 3 teachers spend time teaching a range of good words to replace 'said'. They might display a collection of better words, use cloze procedure, cartoons or shared writing sessions. At the end of the year, much of the work is forgotten as books and pupils disappear for the summer. When pupils move up into the next year, teachers often need to start again from scratch. Of course we need to repeat and consolidate vocabulary, but we can save each other time and effort by building on what has already been done.

A *Word robbery book* (which might also be called *Word relay book* or *Word swag bag*) is a special book (sketch book size is ideal, or it might be a loose-leaf folder) which moves up from class to class with the pupil (hence 'relay'). New words can be added to existing lists or new collections created. Teachers can give pupils ready-made word banks as well as allowing pupils to create their own.

The book is not a substitute for using a thesaurus, but acts as a quick reference tool during writing sessions. Pupils become very familiar with the contents and organisation of their own book. This means they can find key words quickly with fewer interruptions during the writing process.

Suggestions for the contents of a *Word robbery book*:

▶ Word 'maps' of common words (see page 38). These can be used for word games like Word tennis (page 35) or I spy. Each teacher can add more sophisticated words to an existing map.

▶ Topic collections in the back. Specialist or technical words for science, history and geography can be listed alphabetically and given, with definitions, for pupils to use whenever a writing task allows.

▶ Words for colours.

▶ Word games or challenges.

▶ Collections of connectives, openers, adverbs.

▶ Words for specific writing tasks.

▶ Words or phrases that have been 'robbed' from the teacher or from books.

1 WORD TENNIS

Organisation

- A game for two players

Resources

- One whiteboard and one whiteboard pen per pupil
- One thesaurus per pupil
- A dice

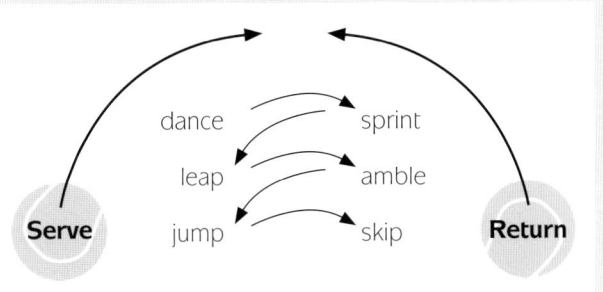

How to play

1. Pupils use an existing word 'map' (see page 38) or spend five minutes with a thesaurus jotting down as many words as they can on a particular theme, e.g. verbs for movement.

2. Pupils then close books, cover jottings and see just how many they can remember by 'serving' and 'returning' words to each other.

3. The pupil who throws the highest number on the dice goes first. 'Shots' can either be oral or written down.

Extension

Pupil 1 serves a word. Pupil 2's return must be a different word with the same meaning.

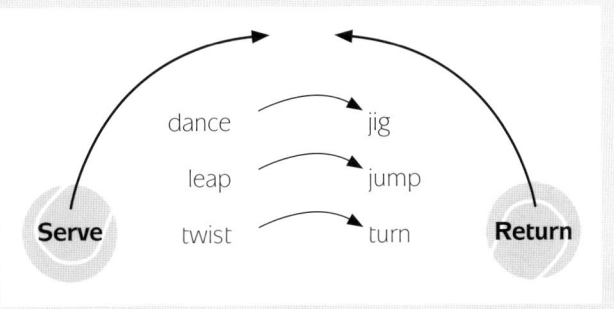

2 CRESCENDO WORDS

Give pupils a word such as 'nice'. Ask them for better words which they then arrange in order from worst to best, or least favourite to favourite with each word written larger than the one before.

nice lovely beautiful splendid glorious

3 WORD BULLSEYES

Give pupils a section of text. Tell them that a certain letter of your choice is the 'target'. They must hunt down and find any words containing that letter and replace the whole word with another (sensible) word.

4 CHALLENGE THREE

Organisation

- The whole class working in pairs or singly

Resources

- A text (at least a page) which the class is reading (any curriculum area)
- One whiteboard and one whiteboard pen per pair/pupil

How to play

1. In pairs, pupils select an object or person from the text.

2. Pupils write down three easy adjectives to describe that object or person.

3. They use a thesaurus to replace their three easy adjectives with three really amazing ones.

4. Pupils read out their three amazing adjectives and 'challenge' another pair in the class to name the object or person.

Examples from the poem 'The Highwayman' (Year 5):

Chosen noun 'blood'
Easy adjectives – thick, red, sticky
Challenge adjectives – viscous, crimson, coagulating

Chosen noun 'Redcoats'
Easy adjectives – mean, nasty, threatening
Challenge adjectives – vulgar, repellent, abusive

5 ADVERB MINI-SAGAS

This game extends a pupil's vocabulary and gives opportunity for role play. It makes a very useful introduction for pupils to write their own fiction. Pupils should be allowed to 'rob' two of your adverbs for their own writing. You can make the act of 'robbery' into a game by forbidding the pupils to 'steal' any of your adverbs for their own use. This guarantees that they will do! You may even turn your back for a moment, before turning quickly round to try to catch them 'stealing'. A further idea is to 'punish' children who have 'stolen' some of your brilliant words by identifying them as having used them in their writing – naming and shaming – 'letting them off this time'! Pupils in Key Stage 2 understand that it is a 'game'.

Organisation

- Whole class

Resources

- List of about five or six impressive adverbs
- Word robbery books (see page 20)

How to play

1 Introduce each adverb. Explain its meaning and make links with words the pupils already know.

Example from a lesson about the Medusa and Perseus (Greek mythology):

The five adverbs we are going to work with today are 'cautiously', 'heroically', 'tentatively', 'frenziedly', 'energetically' and 'triumphantly'.

'Cautiously' comes from the word cautious and it means … ? Now, show me you understand the word by looking around the room 'cautiously'.

'Heroically'. Do we know what a hero is? This adverb comes from that word. Now stand as you imagine a hero would stand.

'Tentatively' means that you hesitate. You are not sure about what you are doing. Reach down and touch something on your desk very 'tentatively'.

'Frenziedly' comes from the word 'frenzy' which means to be going madly at something. Imagine that you are the Medusa and your hair is made up entirely of snakes. Show me the snakes hissing and moving 'frenziedly'.

'Energetically'. Can you spot the link to the word energy? What do you think it means? Now, jump on the spot 'energetically'.

'Triumphantly' means that you have succeeded in your task and feel really pleased because you have 'triumphed'. Show me a 'triumphant' expression.

2 Use the five words in a mini-saga. Pupils act out each stage of the mini-saga as you tell it. (Actions and freeze frames only. Restrict sound effects to certain adverbs!)

Example mini saga:

Cautiously, Perseus edged his way towards the Gorgons' lair.

Heroically, the intrepid adventurer clutched his sword and shield tightly.

Tentatively, he positioned his shield so that he could catch Medusa's reflection.

Frenziedly, the snakes on her head began to hiss as Perseus approached – closer and closer.

Energetically, he began to slash the air with his sharp-edged weapon.

Triumphantly, he hacked off Medusa's head and held it high.

6 MUSICAL VERBS

This game increases a pupil's vocabulary and their knowledge of synonyms.

Organisation

- A whole class or team (minimum number 16) game. Pupils are divided into two teams of equal numbers

Resources

- One whiteboard and one whiteboard pen per pupil
- List of suitable verbs/phrases
- Sufficient chairs for ONE team

How to play

1. Choose two common verbs frequently used by pupils in their writing. Write them on the board and add lists of alternative verbs/verb phrases beneath. Make the lists as challenging as possible. You may prefer to give the past tense of verbs.

2. Without showing anyone else, pupils choose a verb/phrase from the list and write it on their whiteboards.

3. Select teams of equal number. One team sits on chairs arranged in a circle or straight line; the other team prepares to walk clockwise round the sitting pupils. Verbs/phrases are held so that others cannot see them.

4. Play short bursts of music. When the music stops, each pupil in the walking team stands opposite a seated pupil. At a signal from you, they 'show and tell' their verbs.

5. If the verbs 'match', i.e. both verbs come from the same category, the pupil standing takes the seat. If not, they remain in the walking team until the next 'stop'. After each 'stop', all seated pupils add a point to their score.

Throughout the game, pupils swap places when their verbs 'match', learning new verbs as the game continues.

Example musical verbs:

EAT	**RUN**	**ANNOY**	**SAID**
devour	sprint	aggravate	mentioned
guzzle	jog	enrage	utttered
chew	speed	irritate	pronounced
masticate	dash	rub salt in the wound	whispered
	gallop	exasperate	breathed
THROW	tear		shouted
hurl		**WALK**	piped up
pitch	**WONDER**	amble	spoke up
heave	admire	stroll	recited
fling	marvel	promenade	preached
propel	gasp with admiration	saunter	cried
toss	gawp at	march	replied
	be overwhelmed by	tramp	
IMPROVE		ramble	
ameliorate	**SHOUT**	stride out	
upgrade	bellow		
enrich	yell		
refurbish	harangue		
transform	scream		
make better	roar		

7 WORD MAPS

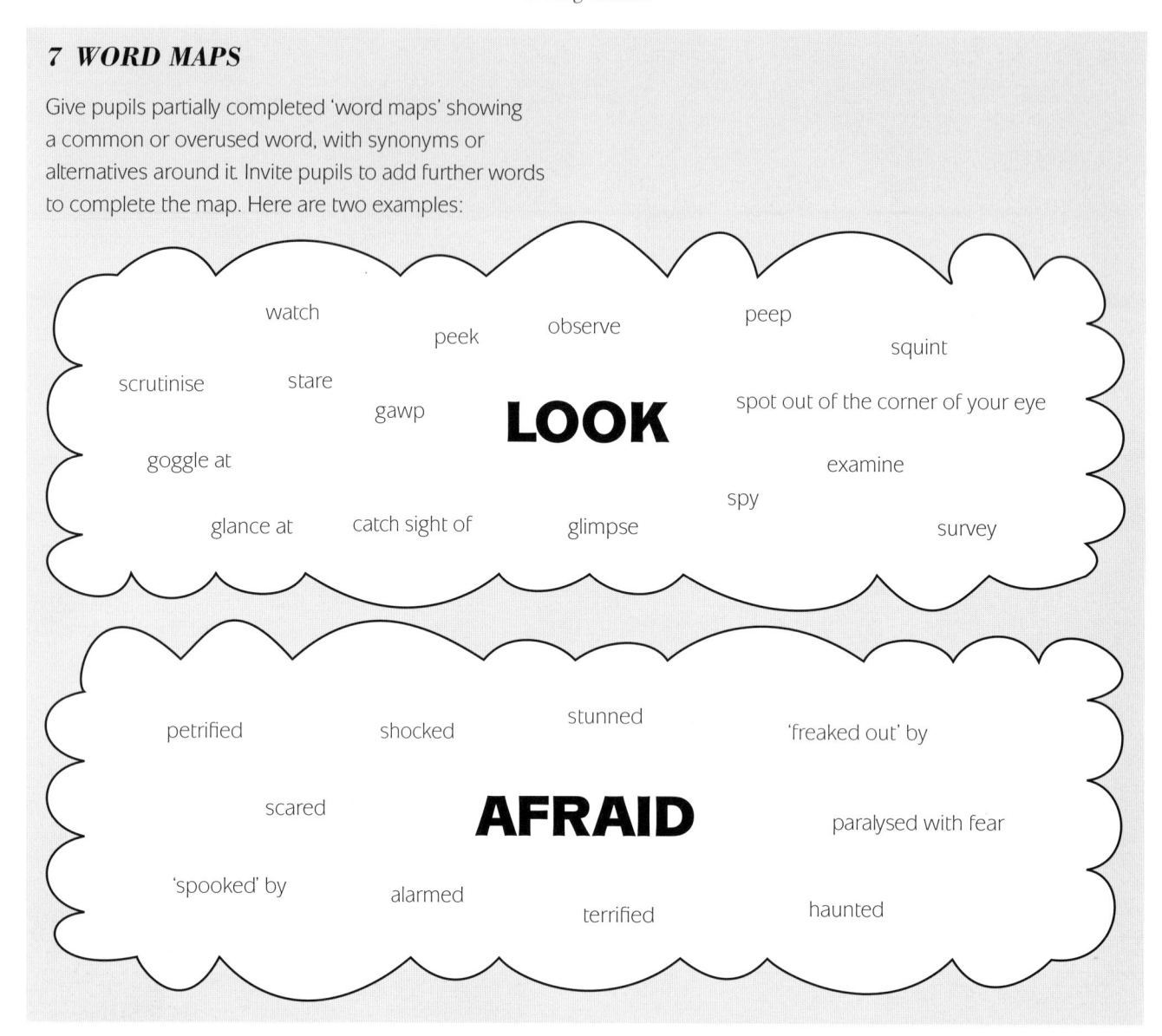

Give pupils partially completed 'word maps' showing a common or overused word, with synonyms or alternatives around it. Invite pupils to add further words to complete the map. Here are two examples:

LOOK: watch, peek, observe, peep, squint, scrutinise, stare, gawp, spot out of the corner of your eye, goggle at, examine, spy, glance at, catch sight of, glimpse, survey

AFRAID: petrified, shocked, stunned, 'freaked out' by, scared, paralysed with fear, 'spooked' by, alarmed, terrified, haunted

WRITING CLINIC 2
Organisation

Assessments show that pupils have difficulty both in organising their writing as a whole and in ordering their ideas within paragraphs. Explaining that writing is like designing and building a house (see page 23) can help pupils to understand the need for text structure and organisation. Below are more suggestions for teaching this aspect of writing.

Pupils often find it helpful to think of these topic or main sentences as 'coat hangers'.

1 COAT HANGERS

Writers need to begin each section or paragraph with a general sentence which:

- tells the reader what the following section will be about
- does not go into specific detail but gives a general outline
- makes links, if possible, to a previous section or paragraph.

Suggested activities

- When reading, draw pupils attention to 'coat hangers'. Explain that we can often work out what a text is about simply by looking at the 'coat hangers'.
- Challenge pupils to find a specific 'coat hanger', e.g. 'I am thinking of a "coat hanger" which tells us about the start of the journey. Who can find it and read it?'
- Pupils might mime or freeze frame 'coat hangers' for other pupils and the teacher to identify.

- Write out specific 'coat hangers' on card and attach to real coat hangers, each given to a different pupil to hold. Ideas for each section or paragraph of a particular writing task can also be written on pieces of card and distributed to pupils in the class. These pupils then 'attach' themselves to the appropriate 'coat hanger'.

- A simple 'fishing' game can be played in guided writing groups. Write a range of ideas for a specific piece of writing on individual pieces of card. These are placed face down on the table. Each pupil in the group is given a relevant topic sentence as a 'coat hanger'. They take it in turns to 'fish' in the 'pool' by picking out an idea card. If they think it 'belongs' to them, they explain why it should be in their paragraph. Any other pupil can argue that it belongs to them instead. If the original pupil 'owns' the idea, they keep it and score a point. If it belongs to another pupil, they hand it over as a free gift. This activity encourages pupils to make links between ideas, to decide what is and what is not relevant, and reinforces how specific texts should be organised. Discussions can be very interesting when more than one pupil claims ownership of the same idea.

PCMs 6 and 7 (see pages 42–43) focus on the sentences at a start of a paragraph that often tell the reader what the paragraph is about.

2 HUMAN PARAGRAPHS

Suggestion 1

Divide a piece of writing into its constituent paragraphs. Give each paragraph a title, then write each title on a piece of card. Repeat so that you have two sets of cards. Two teams of pupils are each given a set of the shuffled paragraph titles. Standing one behind the other, having sorted out what they think is the best order for the paragraphs, each pupil gives their paragraph title and explains why they have put it there. Differences in team choices, if any, can be explored, questions can be put by other pupils and votes taken about the 'best' order.

Example, writing about a mythological creature:

Lair (where it lives)	Stories about it
Appearance	Strange powers
Its name and the culture it is found in	

Suggestion 2

Sentences for one paragraph are written on individual cards and given to a group of pupils. The pupils decide the best order for these, take a sentence card each and form a line at the front of the class in their order. The rest of the class, working in pairs, may also be given the same sentences to discuss and order. It is useful to have the 'human paragraph' at the front of the class as a focus so that the order can be changed easily, ideas added and taken away.

The 'human paragraph' can be used to teach pupils about the structure and organisation of paragraphs in the following ways:

- Insert an idea belonging to another paragraph. Teach pupils to spot the 'odd one out' and remove it.

- Repeat the same idea in a different way. Teach pupils not to repeat ideas unnecessarily by 'throwing out' the repetition.

- Always include a 'coat hanger'. Teach pupils to recognise the main sentence and identify the words which make it general rather than specific.

- Encourage pupils to discuss and justify their chosen sequence of sentences.

- Start sentences with the same word. Teach pupils to link ideas by finding different ways to start sentences and to refer to the same thing using different words, e.g. *She, this creature, the Medusa, according to Greek legend.*

- Have a connective 'board' with connective words and phrases stuck on it which pupils can take off for use in their paragraph.

- Allow the 'human paragraph' a choice of just two connectives/connective phrases. Teach pupils to choose them well and not just to follow a formula, e.g. *moreover, in addition, as well as.*

- Include simple sentences which lack detail. Encourage pupils to expand their ideas and insert whiteboards with extra detail.

PCMs 4 and 5 (see pages 40–41) can be used to help pupils think about why text is organised into paragraphs, and which sentences belong in a particular paragraph.

Name _____   Class _____

PCM 4

Paragraph party 1

A paragraph, 'Feeding your rabbit', is having a party. All the sentences below want to be invited.

- Which sentences do not belong at the party?
- Which sentence is the most important and should go first?
- Which order should the other sentences be put in?
- ONE extra 'guest' is allowed. Choose one from the Guest list and put it at the start of a sentence.
- Write out your paragraph about 'Feeding your rabbit'.

Sentences

| Rabbits like to be kept warm and dry. |

| It is important to give your rabbit the right food. |

| A rabbit must be taken to a vet to have its claws clipped. |

| Your pet needs a mixture of fresh and dried food. |

| Make sure it has a choice of carrots, lettuce and other green vegetables. |

| Always provide fresh water every day. |

Guest list

| finally | | firstly | | next | | also |

Name _____ Class _____

PCM 5
Paragraph party 2

A paragraph, 'The strange powers of the Medusa' is holding a party. All of the sentences below are hoping to be invited.

- Which sentences do not belong at the party?
- Which sentences are repeated and which of the two should be allowed in?
- Which sentence is the most important and should go first?
- Which sentence is last to arrive and goes at the end?
- Decide the order of the other sentences.
- TWO extra 'guests' are allowed. Choose two from the Guest list and put them at the start of two sentences.
- Write your paragraph about the Medusa's strange powers:

_____
_____
_____
_____
_____

Sentences

| She was a character that you would not want to meet. |
| She lived with her sisters in a cave at the very end of the world. |
| The Medusa was one of the most powerful and feared creatures. |
| She could turn any man who looked at her to stone. |
| She had snakes on her head which warned her if anyone approached. |
| If you so much as gazed at her once, you would be turned to stone. |
| She was quite ordinary in some ways. |

Guest list

| meanwhile | unfortunately | finally | for instance | firstly | also | however |
| eventually | in addition | on the other hand | whereas | not only | moreover | next |

Name _____   Class _____

PCM 6

Coat hangers 1 (Fiction)

'Coat hangers' are sentences at the beginning of each section which tell us about the sentences that follow.

- The 'coat hangers' below have got muddled up and separated from the sections they go with.
- Draw lines to link each coat hanger to the correct section.
- Underline the 'coat hanger' words which helped you decide.

Coat hangers

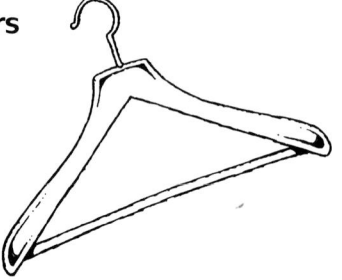

Sections

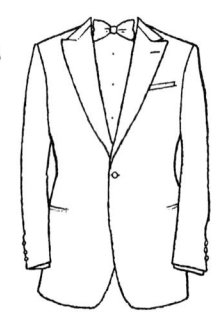

Coat hangers	Sections
One day, his mother told Richard that he would have to sort out his wardrobe once and for all.	As soon as he heard about the latest Manchester United strip, Richard would beg his parents to give him extra jobs. This meant he could earn more money. Straight away he would add the shorts and top to his collection.
Richard's wardrobe was just not big enough for all his clothes.	He could never find his uniform. It was always creased and he often ended up wearing odd socks!
He had enough football kit for a whole team.	He had so many pairs of shoes, coats and T-shirts that his mother had lost count. Every birthday he was given more.
Every morning, before school, Richard had the same problem.	First he put shoes in boxes, then took all clothes that were too small. He put them to one side to be recycled.

Name _____ Class _____

PCM 7

Coat hangers 2 (Non-fiction)

'Coat hangers' are sentences at the beginning of each section which tell us about the rest of the paragraph.

- The 'coat hangers' below have got muddled up and separated from the sections they go with.
- Draw lines to link each coat hanger to the correct section.
- Underline the 'coat hanger' words which helped you decide.

Coat hangers

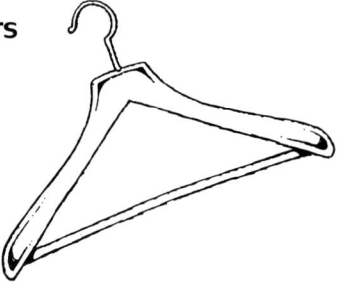

Sections

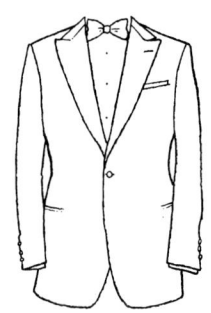

Coat hangers	Sections
Different objects have different densities and this explains why some float and some sink.	A huge submarine will float as well as a small leaf. The important factor is not how large an object is but how dense it is.
Forces are at work all the time in the world around us.	When we swim our bodies feel lighter. This is because our mass is partly supported by the upward thrust of the water. This is called buoyancy.
Water also exerts an upward push on an object.	For example, a leaf is less dense than a stone. Its mass is spread over a larger area. The stone's mass is concentrated in a small area. The leaf floats but the stone sinks because it is denser.
The size of the object is not important.	To understand how we can swim in water, why ships float and what makes oil such a problem when it escapes from ships, we need to know more about upthrust and buoyancy.

Writing clinics

WRITING CLINIC 3
Clauses and connectives

Assessments show that pupils forget to use connective words and phrases to link sentences and clauses within sentences. They also find it difficult to alter the order of clauses within sentences for variety, e.g. 'The dog barked loudly whenever he heard a noise.' 'Whenever he heard a noise, the dog barked loudly.'

This section provides ideas for classroom games focusing on clauses and connectives.

1 CONNECTIVE CRICKET

This is a popular game with pupils in Key Stage 1 and Key Stage 2, and is suitable for literacy and topic lessons.

- It helps pupils to understand complex sentences.
- It teaches subordination.
- It highlights the role of subordinating connectives.
- It encourages flexibility in the use of sentence structure.

Organisation

- Two pupils to hold whiteboards at the front of the class (this role particularly suits less confident pupils)
- A team of four, five, six or more to 'bat'
- The rest of the class as 'bowlers'

Resources

- A 'batting' chair at the front of the classroom
- One whiteboard and one whiteboard pen per pupil
- A sentence opener on one whiteboard
- A connective of your choice on a second whiteboard

How to play

1 Ask two pupils to hold the two whiteboards with your sentence opener and your connective in front of the class.

2 Ask all pupils to complete the sentence opener provided by writing an ending on their whiteboards.

Example:

The teacher came into the room whenever ...
  the bell rang.
  the class was noisy.
  break time was over.

3 Select a team to bat. The pupils in the team line up on one side, each holding their whiteboard endings.

4 When the class 'bowls' (i.e. reads aloud the displayed opener and connective) the first pupil in the batting team runs to the batting chair and reads out their ending. Immediately the class 'bowls' again.

5 Continue until all members of the team have been in to 'bat'.

6 Runs are scored for reaching the batting chair (in time) and for supplying an ending which makes sense.

Extend the game: the two pupils holding the sentence opener and the connective can shout 'SWITCH IT!' and change places. The 'bowlers', i.e. the class, must then read the sentence the other way round, i.e. *Whenever the teacher came into the room ...*

This can alter the meaning of the 'run' (sentence) so that the ending is more amusing or no longer makes sense. The batting team should line up at the front so that the meaning of 'runs' can be discussed by the class at the end of the innings.

Once the pupils are confident with the game, appropriate use of the comma to separate clauses can also be emphasised, with the 'bowlers' reading aloud the sentence opening and the connective and drawing the appropriate punctuation in the air.

Examples of 'starters' for 'Connective cricket'

1 *The boy played for his team   whenever ...*
   ➡ *Whenever the boy played for his team ...*

2 *She watched television   while ...*
   ➡ *While she watched television ...*

3 *The two children were involved in an argument   because ...*
   ➡ *Because the two children were involved in an argument ...*

4 *They left the party   when ...*
   ➡ *When they left the party ...*

5 *The unfortunate dog dashed into the road   before ...*
   ➡ *Before the unfortunate dog dashed into the road ...*

6 *They liked to play with the new boy   although ...*
   ➡ *Although they liked to play with the new boy ...*

Writing clinics

Cross curricular examples:

Science
Jenner tested his vaccine on lots of people because ...
➡ *Because Jenner tested his vaccine on lots of people ...*

History
In 1939 Britain declared war on Germany after ...
➡ *After Britain declared war on Germany in 1939 ...*

2 CONNECTIVE WEDDINGS

This game is for Key Stage 2 pupils. It:

▶ introduces pupils to a range of connective 'partners'

▶ helps pupils to write more complex sentences

▶ allows for peer and self improvement of sentences.

Organisation

▶ Pupils either singly or in pairs with whiteboards and whiteboard pens

Resources

▶ Board or interactive whiteboard with connective pairs written down and (optional) graphics, e.g. wedding ring or bells

▶ One whiteboard and one whiteboard pen per pupil or pair

How to play

1 You might choose to begin with the following:

'We are gathered here today to witness the joining together of that lovely connective couple "not only" and "but also". If anyone here has any good grammatical reason why these two connective phrases should NOT be joined together, let them speak out now or forever use them in EVERY piece of writing!'

2 Pupils make up sentences combining the connectives. Sentences can be relevant to whichever current writing task the class is working on.

3 Select pupils to read out their 'wedding' sentence.

4 The class is asked to suggest a 'wedding present' for each happy connective couple. It might be an adjective, a more interesting verb or more advanced punctuation. The intention is to improve the sentence further.

Examples of connective 'partners'

Not only ... but also ..., e.g. Not only was the Gorgon the ugliest creature Perseus had ever seen but she was also the most dangerous.

If ... then ..., e.g. If you will tidy your room, then I will let you go out to play.

Then ... but ..., e.g. Then they scored again, but their triumph was short-lived.

Then ... so ..., e.g. Then they took the dog for a walk so it could have its daily run in the park.

Whenever ... or ..., e.g. Whenever they went to the far side of the park, they had to 'leg it' back quickly, or they would miss the bus.

Either ... or ..., e.g. Either you tidy up your room this minute or I will stop your pocket money.

Example of 'wedding present' suggestions:

Original sentence: *Not only was George the most loathsome giant Jack had ever seen but he was also one of the most powerful as he could pick up a mountain and throw it to land over five miles away.*

Suggestions of 'wedding presents' to improve it:

alliteration – gruesome George
punctuation – comma after 'seen'
punctuation – ellipsis after 'could'.
'wow' verb – replace 'throw' with 'hurl'

WRITING CLINIC 4
Sentence openers

Assessments show that pupils find it difficult to use a range of sentence openers to add detail and variety. 'Openers mix and match' teaches pupils a range of adverbial phrases of time, place and manner.

OPENERS MIX AND MATCH

A game for Key Stage 1 and Key Stage 2 pupils. It:

- extends pupils' vocabulary
- helps pupils to vary sentence 'starts'
- encourages concentration and memory skills.

Organisation

- Whole class

Resources

- A selection of sentence openers (time, place or manner) typed/written on the board or interactive whiteboard

How to play

1. Using PCM 8 as a guide, display a collection of sentence openers on the board or interactive whiteboard. These should all be either of time, place or manner. For each opener, there should be another that has the same meaning.

2. Invite individual pupils to the board to link a pair of sentence openers with a straight line. Each time they correctly identify a pair, they use one of the openers to begin a sentence. They then challenge the rest of the class to use the other opener to begin a different sentence.

PCM 8

Sentence opener collections

Time

Instantaneously	At that precise	Later	Frequently
A moment later	moment	Following that	Often
In a short while	Promptly	Subsequently	Regularly
Before long	Instantly	A while later	Time and time again
Immediately	At once	After some time	Repeatedly
In an instant	Without warning	At last	In quick succession
Quick as a flash	Before you could say	Late in the day	Time after time
Simultaneously	Jack Robinson	In the nick of time	
Suddenly	Straight away	As an afterthought	Infrequently
Abruptly		At the last minute	Occasionally
In no time at all	Earlier		Scarcely ever
Seconds later	Previously		Rarely
Just then	With time to spare		Once in a while
	In good time		Once in a blue moon

Order

Firstly	In the first place	Finally	Secondly
Initially	Primarily	In conclusion	After that
To start with	From the word go	In the end	Next
To begin with		When all is said and done	Then
Originally		At the close	
As a start			

Place

Behind	At the side	Beneath	As well as
To the rear of	Adjacent to	Under	Moreover
At the back of	To the left	Below	In addition
Far off	To the right	At the bottom	Plus
	Close by		Furthermore
Before	Nearby	Above	
Ahead	Level with	High up	
In front of	Next to	On top of	
In the distance		Overhead	

WRITING CLINIC 5
Punctuation

Assessments show that pupils' problems with punctuation often follow a pattern. They forget basic sentence demarcation when concentrating on a range of other writing skills. When they start to use other punctuation they use it too freely to begin with. They find it difficult to understand where to use commas to separate clauses. Added to this, pupils often resent being asked to edit and re-draft work, which would give them the perfect opportunity to correct and insert appropriate punctuation. In this section we provide ideas for a number of classroom activities designed to improve the accuracy and consistency of a pupil's punctuation.

1 COMMANDER COMMA

Introduce the class to Commander Comma. Before they write, pupils should draw Commander Comma (or their own version) on planning sheets to remind them that they need to use as many pieces of punctuation correctly as possible. Use a simplified version for younger pupils.

2 BEAT THE MUSIC

A class challenge which is great for working on all aspects of punctuation, including using commas to separate clauses.

How to play

1 Put a short piece of unpunctuated text on the board (two or three sentences). Explain to the class that you think they will not be able to punctuate the writing correctly before the music stops, even if they work together as one team.

2 With a piece of music playing quietly in the background, the first volunteer comes to the board and puts in a piece of missing punctuation.

3 Before sitting down, they 'teach' the rest of the class, explaining what they have inserted and why. This pupil then chooses another to come to the board.

4 This is repeated until either the music stops, or the writing is fully punctuated. If the pupils complete the punctuation before the end of the music the class has 'won'. If not, the teacher has won. (Ensure that the class 'wins' most of the time!)

Although pupils may make mistakes, make no comment. Another pupil will usually spot the error and change it. At the end of the activity, discuss any issues arising. Pupils then read the sentences, saying and drawing the punctuation in the air with their fingers.

3 HUMAN PUNCTUATION

Sentences (one word or clause per whiteboard) are made at the front by a group of pupils. Other pupils, holding whiteboards with punctuation on, can be inserted into the relevant place, moved around and substituted to show how punctuation contributes to meaning and supports the reader.

4 PUNCTUATION FRUIT SALAD

- Reinforces the need for **.** **!** or **?** at the ends of sentences.
- Helps pupils to recognise which of the three to use.

Organisation

- Whole class

Resources

- One whiteboard and one whiteboard pen per pupil
- Whiteboard at the front of the class

How to play

1 Draw the three pieces of punctuation (full stop, question mark and exclamation mark) on the board. The game can be introduced as Punctuation fruit salad/Punctuation Grand Prix/Punctuation Olympics or any other name.

2 Explain that you will give one piece of punctuation to each pupil. They must draw it on their whiteboards.

3 Write on the board (or say) a selection of sentences. Pupils who think that their piece of punctuation should complete the sentence stand up and hold up their whiteboards.

WRITING CLINIC 6
Different text types

It is often helpful to give pupils prompts to remind them about the key features of different text types, so that they can use these features in their writing. You can photocopy and cut out the photocopy masters 9 and 10 to use as reminders. They can be used for display or use as bookmarks.

PCM 9 — Text types 1

RECOUNTS should have:	EXPLANATION TEXTS should have:
When? Who? Where? What? Why? Use: Paragraphs, Time connectives, Past tense. Give: An opinion	1 a Headings b Sub-headings 2 Definition 3 Paragraphs 4 Conclusion Include: Flow charts, Diagrams. Use: Connectives, Present tense, Action verbs, Technical words
STORIES should have:	A NEWSPAPER REPORT should have:
A good story opening to grab the reader's attention – where? when? atmosphere? Two characters and what they are like. Complications – something exciting happens. A good ending – ties up loose ends and gives the reader something to think about. Make sure you: Use paragraphs. Balance action, dialogue and description. Use full range of punctuation . ? ! , " " ( ) … – : ;	1 HUMONGOUS headline – alliterative if possible 2 1st paragraph – who? what? when? 3 2nd paragraph – description, why? 4 A quote from a person, e.g. Mrs Muddle (21) of South Tepton said yesterday, '…'. 5 A range of tenses 6 Conclusion – what will happen now?

PCM 10 — Text types 2

DISCUSSION WRITING should have:	LETTERS should have:	INTERVIEWS should:	PLAYSCRIPTS should:
Opening statement – what will be covered? Mixture of fact/opinion. Arguments for. Arguments against. Summary. Use: Paragraphs. Link connectives, e.g. in addition, on the other hand. Questions. Active and passive verbs.	1 Address 2 Date 3 A greeting, e.g. 'Dear…' 4 Clear opening statement 5 Organised ideas in paragraphs 6 Balance of facts, feelings and opinions. Decide if formal/informal and use appropriate language 7 An appropriate ending Use: 1st person, e.g. I am writing. Mainly present tense. Connectives in complex sentences. Questions.	Ask open/ questions. Ask questions in a sensible order. Pick up key words from question in answers. Have an introduction – welcome. Have a conclusion – thank you. Use: Chatty style, e.g. writing as people speak, slang, etc. Range of tenses.	Have stage directions (not in complete sentences). Have names of characters on left. Have instructions (adverbs) for characters in brackets following name, e.g. (nervously). Show character. Move action along through stage directions.
REPORTS should have:	INSTRUCTIONS should have:	INFORMATION TEXTS should have:	BIOGRAPHIES should have:
Introduction – what you are writing about. Sections/paragraphs each covering a different area. Conclusion. Use: Present tense. Passive. Technical words. Questions. Sub-headings. Tables/diagrams. Range of resources, e.g. books, internet, CDs.	Title with a goal, e.g. 'How to make a cake'. Clear list of materials and equipment. Sequenced, numbered steps of what to do. Headings/sub-headings, bullet points. Command verbs, e.g. cut, stir. Chronological order. Diagram with labels.	Title/heading. Opening statement/general introduction. Use: Sub-headings. Passive tense. Pictures/drawings. Table of information.	Introduction and conclusion. Past tense for things that have happened. Time connectives, e.g. later on, after that. Complex sentences. Chronological order.

PCM 9

Text types 1

RECOUNTS should have:

- When?
- Who?
- Where?
- What?
- Why?

Use:

- Paragraphs
- Time connectives
- Past tense

Give:

- An opinion

STORIES should have:

- A good story opening to grab the reader's attention – where? when? atmosphere?
- Two characters and what they are like
- Complications – something exciting happens
- A good ending – ties up loose ends and gives the reader something to think about

Make sure you:

- Use paragraphs
- Balance action, dialogue and description
- Use full range of punctuation
  . ? ! , " " ( ) … – : ;

EXPLANATION TEXTS should have:

1 a Headings
  b Sub-headings

2 Definition

3 Paragraphs

4 Conclusion

Include:

- Flow charts
- Diagrams

Use:

- Connectives
- Present tense
- Action verbs
- Technical words

A NEWSPAPER REPORT should have:

1 HUMUNGOUS headline – alliterative if possible

2 1st paragraph – who? what? when?

3 2nd paragraph – description, why?

4 A quote from a person, e.g. Mrs Muddle (21) of South Tepton said yesterday, '…'

5 A range of tenses

6 Conclusion – what will happen now?

PCM 10

Text types 2

DISCUSSION WRITING
should have:
- Opening statement – what will be covered?
- Mixture of fact/opinion
- Arguments for
- Arguments against
- Summary

Use:
- Paragraphs
- Link connectives, e.g. in addition, on the other hand
- Questions
- Active and passive verbs

LETTERS
should have:
1. Address
2. Date
3. A greeting, e.g. 'Dear …'
4. Clear opening statement
5. Organised ideas in paragraphs
6. Balance of facts, feelings and opinions. Decide if formal/informal and use appropriate language
7. An appropriate ending

Use:
- 1st person, e.g. I am writing
- Mainly present tense
- Connectives in complex sentences
- Questions

INTERVIEWS
should:
- Ask 'open' questions
- Ask questions in a sensible order
- Pick up key words from question in answers
- Have an introduction – welcome
- Have a conclusion – thank you

Use:
- 'Chatty' style, e.g. writing as people speak, slang, etc.
- Range of tenses

PLAYSCRIPTS
should:
- Have stage directions (not in complete sentences)
- Have names of characters on left
- Have instructions (adverbs) for characters in brackets following name, e.g. (nervously)
- Show character
- Move action along through stage directions

REPORTS
should have:
- Introduction – what you are writing about
- Sections/paragraphs each covering a different area
- Conclusion

Use:
- Present tense
- Passive
- Technical words
- Questions
- Sub-headings
- Tables/diagrams
- Range of resources, e.g. books, internet, CDs

INSTRUCTIONS
should have:
- Title with a goal, e.g. 'How to make a cake'
- Clear list of materials and equipment
- Sequenced, numbered steps of what to do
- Headings/sub-headings, bullet points
- Command verbs, e.g. cut, stir
- Chronological order
- Diagram with labels

INFORMATION TEXTS
should have:
- Title/heading
- Opening statement/ general introduction

Use:
- Sub-headings
- Passive tense
- Pictures/drawings
- Table of information

BIOGRAPHIES
should have:
- Introduction and conclusion
- Past tense for things that have happened
- Time connectives, e.g. later on, after that
- Complex sentences
- Chronological order

In this section we look at ways in which pupils can carry out peer and self assessment.

Peer and self assessment

Pupils need to be able to assess their own and others' writing through self and peer assessment because:

- it reinforces their understanding of whatever is being taught and of the targets they are working towards
- it gives them thinking time so that they can stand back from and reflect on their writing
- it helps them to see where changes need to be made
- it gives them a focus to discuss their writing with their teacher
- it helps them to appreciate the progress they have made.

Annotating and highlighting models of writing provided by the teacher:

- enables pupils to identify success criteria in written models
- gives pupils opportunities to practise evaluation of writing
- stimulates further ideas for writing
- enables pupils to compare different qualities of texts.

Peer assessment of writing helps pupils because:

- discussion with a writing 'buddy' enables pupils to evaluate and refine their original ideas
- it provides writers with an audience whose responses, and need for clarification, help the writer to improve

- a 'buddy' is often more objective in identifying where and how writing might be improved.

Responding to success criteria

Success criteria and targets may be written in pupils' books or simply numbered. During lessons, pupils can show whether they think they have made good, partial or little progress against each target by:

- giving 'on-the-spot' feedback, e.g. holding thumbs up, straight or down
- drawing a smiley, non-committal or gloomy face
- giving each target a mark between 0 and 10
- using a green, orange or red traffic light symbol next to each target.

Using the Photocopy Masters to analyse and assess writing

Photocopy Master 11 (see page 54) gives an example of a writing 'buddy' agreement. It is designed to lay down agreed ground rules when pupils are marking or assessing each other's work.

Peer or self assessment can be an effective way of focusing a pupil's attention on handwriting standards. Depending on the class, your school policy of teaching handwriting and the amount of practice pupils have had, you want pupils to be able to review the following independently:

Peer and *self assessment*

- Letter formation
- Joins
- Size and spacing
- Orientation (position on lines)

To make a self assessment more appealing, think of a suitable theme. A sea theme is used in the example on PCM 12 (page 55). This five-minute assessment activity should be used for small samples of handwriting. Ask pupils to choose a short two- or three-line section of their handwriting. Keep the sample to this length otherwise their editing can make the work untidy or illegible. Tell pupils to carry out a 'sea search' of their handwriting sample.

Pupils can assess their own handwriting or that of a 'buddy'. Self assessment raises a pupil's awareness of their own bad habits or carelessness. A 'buddy', on the other hand, is often better at picking up anomalies.

Photocopy Masters 13–21 (see pages 56–69) provide a selection of different ways for pupils, in pairs or individually, to analyse and assess a range of writing models. Photocopy Master 14 gives ideas to help pupils carry out self and peer assessment of handwriting.

Photocopy Master 17 ('Our writing workout') can be used by teachers and 'buddy' writing pairs when analysing and assessing different types of writing. Not all sections need to be completed. Decide on the most appropriate for the piece of writing being assessed.

Photocopy Masters 18–20 give pupils opportunities to practise assessing different types of writing. Photocopy Master 18 ('Help needed with our report!') relates to persuasive writing and focuses on selecting appropriate reasons to back up views. Photocopy Master 19 ('The classroom at night) focuses on assessing fiction writing, and PCM 20 ('SpikoSpeedoShoes') relates to assessing persuasive letters.

Pupils can collect their own tips to improve a piece of writing on Photocopy Master 21 ('Terrific tips for a writing workout!').

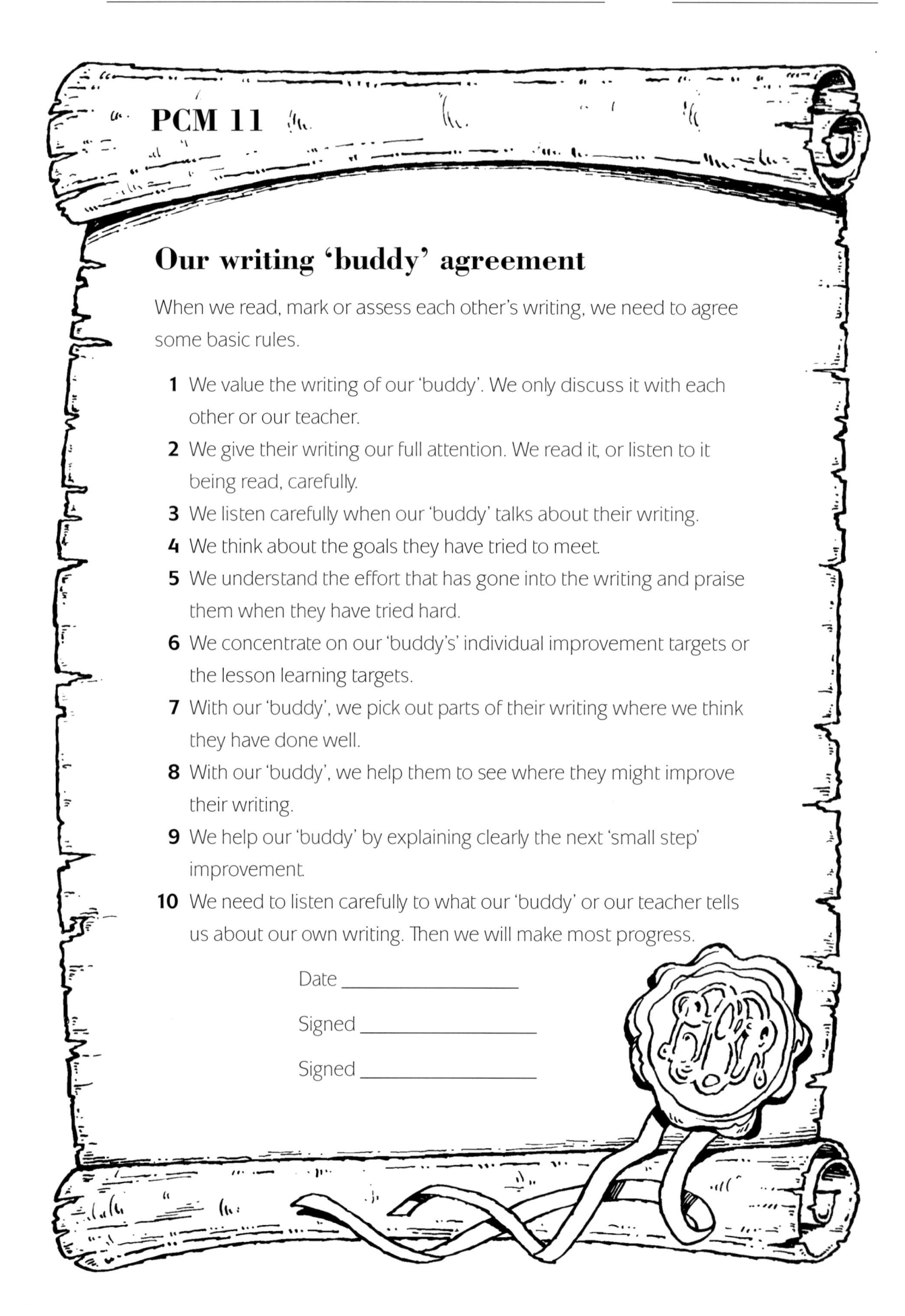

Name _____   Class _____

PCM 11

Our writing 'buddy' agreement

When we read, mark or assess each other's writing, we need to agree some basic rules.

1. We value the writing of our 'buddy'. We only discuss it with each other or our teacher.
2. We give their writing our full attention. We read it, or listen to it being read, carefully.
3. We listen carefully when our 'buddy' talks about their writing.
4. We think about the goals they have tried to meet.
5. We understand the effort that has gone into the writing and praise them when they have tried hard.
6. We concentrate on our 'buddy's' individual improvement targets or the lesson learning targets.
7. With our 'buddy', we pick out parts of their writing where we think they have done well.
8. With our 'buddy', we help them to see where they might improve their writing.
9. We help our 'buddy' by explaining clearly the next 'small step' improvement.
10. We need to listen carefully to what our 'buddy' or our teacher tells us about our own writing. Then we will make most progress.

Date _____

Signed _____

Signed _____

PCM 12

Sea search

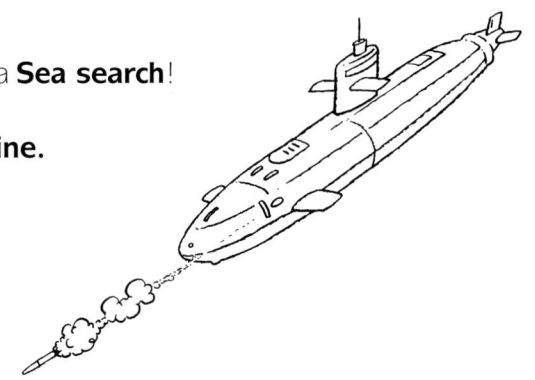

On a short piece of your ordinary handwriting carry out a **Sea search**!

Submarines 'attack' any letters not resting on the line.

In your handwriting, search out any letters or words that are not resting on the line and draw an arrow → underneath them. Next time take more care not to be 'sunk'!

Sharks 'bite' any letters not 'holding on' to one another correctly.

Your teacher will give you 'joins' to look for. If you spot a careless join, draw the shark ∿ in between the two letters.

Practise the join again three times at the bottom of your work.

Jellyfish 'sting' letters which are bigger or smaller than the letters around them.

(Of course capital letters are MEANT to be larger!)

Look for letters which are too big or too small. This includes:

- **s** at the beginning of words
- letters in the middle of words
- **y g j** and **p** which are too long
- **d t l k** which are too tall.

If you find one, 'sting' it by putting a jellyfish on top ∩. Write the word again at the bottom of your work making sure letters are the correct size.

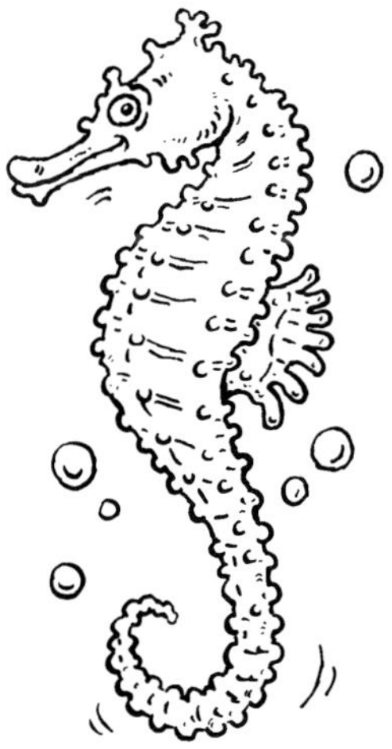

Seahorses search for silly spaces.

Look at the spaces between words and letters. Are some too big or too small? If you find one draw the seahorse symbol ㄹ.

Name _____   Class _____

PCM 13

Analysing and assessing writing: examples

> Imagine a creature called a Tongo Lizard.
>
> It is an endangered creature, which means that very few remain and it may become extinct.
>
> An information book about endangered creatures is being prepared.
>
> Your task is to write the page about the Tongo Lizard.
>
> You can make up the information using your imagination.
>
> English Key Stage 2, *Writing and spelling. Writing Test Shorter Task*, QCA, 2006

This is what two writers, Helen and Naseem, have written.

WRITER: Helen (H)

The Tongo lizard is very rare it lives in the desert and it builds its nest under rocks and in sand. But it is not seen very often because it is yellow and grey and it has sharp claws and bright red spots on its neck eagles try to eat it so there are not many left. It has a long tongue and it likes to eat ants and worms. It is a very special lizard but a bit weird.

WRITER: Naseem (N)

The Tongo lizard, of the Amazon Basin, is an endangered species the only lizard to survive from prehistoric times.

Its usual habitat is high in the tree canopy, where it hides from predators, using large leaves for protection. The Tongo's nest is also constructed here.

These unique creatures are omnivores and consume prey easily as they have dangerously sharp teeth. However, their favourite delicacies are crocodile eggs, young armadillos and rodents.

Tongo lizards are bright turquoise with long tails, black circular markings and very dry, scaly skin. Males have a multicoloured fin which acts as a warning when they are under attack.

These rare animals are in serious danger of becoming extinct unless we act now to save these beautiful and unusual reptiles.

Name _____ Class _____

PCM 14a

Your chance to assess writing!

Read what Helen and Naseem have written about the Tongo Lizard on PCM 13. Look more closely at parts that are good and the parts that could be improved.

With your partner, follow the instructions in each box below.

WRITING: Helen	WRITING: Naseem
Using connectives Circle the connectives Helen has mainly used: and but so when because if where which although who Any other connectives? _____	**Using connectives** Circle the connectives Naseem has mainly used: and but so when because if where which although who Any other connectives? _____
Amazing adjectives Find examples to write below and decide whether they are: ▶ simple _____ ▶ good _____ ▶ amazing _____	**Amazing adjectives** Find examples to write below and decide whether they are: ▶ simple _____ ▶ good _____ ▶ amazing _____
Points Helen's writing is not divided into sections. What points does she make? **1** Where it lives **2** What _____ **3** _____	**Sections** Naseem's writing is divided into ☐ sections. Think of a title for each. **1** _____ **2** _____ **3** _____ **4** _____ **5** _____ **6** _____
Punctuation Circle below the punctuation Helen uses: ▶ full stops and capital letters correct ▶ ! ? and commas in a list ▶ commas within sentences ▶ - : ; 's	**Punctuation** Circle below the punctuation Naseem uses: ▶ full stops and capital letters correct ▶ ! ? and commas in a list ▶ commas within sentences ▶ - : ; 's

Name _____ Class _____

PCM 14b

Your chance to assess writing! (continued)

Read what Helen and Naseem have written about the Tongo Lizard on PCM 13.

Put **H** or **N** next to the statement below which you think describes Helen's or Naseem's writing best.

Description

☐ I describe the lizard by just listing things about it.

☐ I go into more detail giving information and reasons.

☐ I give a very vivid description of the animal so my reader can imagine what it is like.

☐ My writing reads like a REAL INFORMATION BOOK in describing many aspects.

Words chosen

☐ I use simple words like *burrow*, *best*, *black* and *red* mostly.

☐ I use better words like *damp*, *favourite* and *habitat*.

☐ I use powerful describing words like *blends*, *dense*, *swampy marshes*.

☐ I use amazing adjectives and some science or specialist words.

Look at the notes you have made about Helen and Naseem and talk about what they need to do next to improve their writing.

PCM 15

Naseem's 'buddy' response sheet

Naseem showed his work to his writing partner, Richard. Richard read it with Naseem and filled in the 'buddy' response sheet below. He looked at the targets their teacher had given Naseem, picked out two things he thought Naseem had done well and suggested one thing he could improve.

I just wanted to say …

Learning opportunity	Activity	Targets for success
Write a short informative description.	Write a page for an information book about the endangered Tongo Lizard.	Give clear explanations. Use interesting describing. Use scientific words.

Richard wrote:

I just wanted to say:

✓ You have used some great describing words like 'turquoise' and multi-coloured.

✓ When you used science words like 'predators' and 'omnivores' your writing sounded like a real information book.

! You explain why it makes its nest where it does but I think you should explain more clearly why the Tongo Lizard is endangered.

Naseem's reply:

Thanks! I forgot to put in why it is threatened. I am going to add … 'These rare creatures are captured by local poachers who use their skins for decorative cloaks.'

Teacher's comments:

Your comments were very helpful, Richard. Naseem, now show me with an * where you are going to put the extra sentence. You have worked hard on your personal target – to organise your ideas into paragraphs. REMEMBER to use hyphens for 'pre-historic' and multi-coloured.

Name _____ Class _____

PCM 16

My 'buddy' response sheet

My 'buddy's' name _____

Learning opportunity	Activity	Targets for success

My 'buddy's' comments:

✓

✓

!

My reply and the changes I will make:

Teacher's comments:

Name _____   Class _____

PCM 17

Our writing workout

Which connectives are mainly used in the writing? **Circle any that you find.** and but so when because if where which although who Any other connectives? _____	**How many different kinds of sentence?** **Tick if you can find any of the following.** ☐ Short simple sentences ☐ Two sentences joined together with 'and', 'but' or 'so' ☐ Complex sentences with a connective ☐ Longer, more complicated sentences with more than one connective
Amazing adjectives or adverbs Find an example and decide whether they are: ▶ Simple _____ ▶ Good _____ ▶ Amazing _____	**What kind of opening does it have?**
How many sections in this piece of writing? **Give each section a title.**	**What do you think of the ending and why?**
Circle the punctuation below if you find correctly used examples in the writing. ▶ full stops and capital letters correct ▶ ! ? and commas in a list ▶ commas within sentences ▶ - : … 's ( )	**How many different ways are used to open sentences? Give examples.**
How well does the writing describe, explain, inform or persuade?	**How well are words and phrases chosen? Write five of the best examples below.**

Name _____   Class _____

PCM 18a

Help needed with our report!

Children at Shovel-It-Down-And-Run Primary School hate lunchtimes! They don't like it when it is wet, they complain that there is no space in the dining room and they would like more games provided in the playground. The head teacher has asked the School Council to write a report suggesting changes and explaining why these would make lunchtimes better.

Some of the reasons we have given are silly.

I think all our reasons are good ones!

Jamie, the Year 6 School Council rep, is not happy with the report.

Rachel, the Year 5 School Council rep, is pleased with what they have written.

They need your help to improve their report. Look at the underlined reasons. If you think they are sensible, circle the star [*]; if not, circle the exclamation mark [!]. For each reason you think is not very good, write a better one at the bottom!

These reasons would improve your report:

1 _____

2 _____

3 _____

4 _____

Name _____ Class _____

PCM 18b

Report by the School Council of Shovel-It-Down-And-Run Primary School

---

5th June 2008

To whom it may concern

Not many pupils at the school enjoy lunchtimes at the moment <u>because they would rather be at home on their own eating their dinner</u> [*] [!]. Lunchtimes are always mentioned in class suggestion boxes. We think our ideas will improve lunchtimes.

There is often a lot of trouble in the playground at lunchtime; this is <u>ALWAYS due to the Y6 children being nasty and bullying others</u> [*] [!]. We need a Friendship Stop where older pupils can wait to help others in trouble or to organise group games. <u>This would give some older pupils more responsibility and mean that younger children, who are feeling lonely, would have a place to go if they wanted someone to play with</u> [*] [!].

Another suggestion would be to provide a box of games equipment like ropes, small balls and skittles. <u>This would give pupils different games to play</u> [*] [!]. At the moment, pupils just charge around the Quiet Area, <u>which is not good as this is not what the Quiet Area is for</u> [*] [!]. Making the playground a better place <u>would mean that children will bring in more games from home</u> [*] [!].

We could also improve the dining hall where we eat our lunch. <u>If it were noisier</u> [*] [!], pupils would not just gollop down their dinners or sandwiches and rush out onto the playground! We could have a screen with messages and school news <u>to stop pupils getting bored while they are queueing up</u> [*] [!]. It takes ages for pupils to be served. We could have a menu board. The choices for that day could be written up so that we could make our minds up before we get to the serving tables. <u>This would save time</u> [*] [!]. Having a menu board <u>would also mean we would always get our first choice</u> [*] [!].

We hope that you will take notice of our ideas.

School Council, Shovel-It-Down-And-Run Primary School

Name _____ Class _____

PCM 19a

The classroom at night

'By day, it was full of children and noise. But at night, when everyone had gone home, it was quite different. At first, locked in by mistake, Sam had thought it would be great fun. But now he was not so sure …'

Your task is to write about what happened to Sam next.

This is what two writers, Helen and Naseem, have written about the classroom at night.

WRITER: Helen (H)

The floor creaked and the wind whistled. It was not very nice because it was very frightening. Paintbrushes in a pot looked like furry animals sam was very frightened the desks were hard, shiny and there were lots of them. A model in the corner looked like a black monster. When sam walked around the floor creaked again like a scurrying mouse he saw his shiny reflection in the window. It made him jump a mile high.

WRITER: Naseem (N)

As he gazed nervously around the classroom, Sam could hear his own heart pounding like a machine. He tried to make out familiar things. What could he see?

Over there, in the corner, that funny shape was a glistening globe which pointed, with a metal finger to all the countries of the world. In the darkness, the whiteboard gleamed whenever the moonlight hit its face. Surrounding him, like a pack of hyenas, desks crouched waiting to pounce.

The smell of polish on desks and cupboards reminded him of the morning when he would walk in to a nice, clean room. He wished it was morning now! Nearby, the strong smell of disinfectant came from the sink.

He could hear nothing except the tick of the classroom clock and, outside, the wind howling like a ghost. He started crying!

Name _____   Class _____

PCM 19b

Read the stories by Helen and Naseem in PMC19a.

Put **H** or **N** next to the statement below which you think describes Helen's or Naseem's writing best.

Description

☐ I describe the classroom by just listing things about it.

☐ I give more detail and include some reference to senses.

☐ I give a vivid description of the classroom including sensory descriptions. I describe Sam's feelings so my reader can imagine what the classroom is like.

☐ My writing describes many aspects of the classroom and creates a sense of mystery.

Words chosen

☐ I use simple words like *soft* and *red* mostly.

☐ I use better words like *dusty*, *creak*, *scurrying*.

☐ I use powerful words to describe the room e.g. *reflecting*, *squatted*, *shadowy*, *swirling*.

☐ I use very well-chosen words effectively e.g. *luminous*, *acrid*, *elongated*.

Put **H** or **N** next to any of the statements below if you can find evidence in
Helen's or Naseem's writing.

Stylistic choices

☐ I sometimes repeat words/phrases because I cannot think of better words.

☐ I use similes ('like a …').

☐ I use alliteration ('**w**ailing **w**ind').

☐ I use personification (make objects appear to be living creatures, e.g. 'desks crouching').

My buddy response sheet

Learning opportunity	Activity	Targets for success
To write a story opening.	Write a description of a classroom at night.	Use interesting adjectives for vivid visual description. Use similes, alliteration and personification.

Name _____ Class _____

PCM 19c

Imagine that you are Helen's or Naseem's teacher. What comments would you put on their writing? Use the sentence starters below to mark their work.

Teacher's comments:
HELEN / **NASEEM** (circle the pupil chosen)
You have tried very hard to
I particularly liked the part(s) where
Try to improve by

✂--

Name _____ Class _____

PCM 19d

Use this blank form when you are marking a friend's writing.

My comments for _____
You have tried very hard to
I particularly liked the part(s) where
Try to improve by

Name _____ Class _____

PCM 20a

SpikoSpeedoShoes

Mark and Joanne are doing this task:

> 'SpikoSpeedoShoes' are the very latest in expensive running shoes. You bought some over a month ago and, although they are very good in some ways, you have had one or two problems.
>
> Your task is to write an e-mail to the company about your 'SpikoSpeedoShoes' asking them to repair the shoes or to give you your money back.

Mark and Joanne have each written an e-mail to the 'SpikoSpeedoShoes' company.

Read Mark's e-mail. Then read Joanne's. With a writing 'buddy', decide what is better about Joanne's e-mail. Then write out a 'Terrific tips for a writing workout' sheet for Mark (see PCM 21).

To: SpikoSpeedoShoes@speedo.co.uk

Cc:

Subject: My new SpikoSpeedoShoes

I tried out spikospeedoshoes and they were really nice to begin with. It is made of nice soft material and they are a brilliant colour but after two weeks the laces snapped and the sole came unstuck I do not think that should happen and I want my money back or the shoes fixing I am sending the shoes back to you in a box

Love Mark

Name _____ Class _____

PCM 20b

You have read Mark's e-mail on PCM20a. Now read Joanne's email on this PCM.

To: SpikoSpeedoShoes@speedo.co.uk

Cc:

Subject: Problems with my new SpikoSpeedoShoes

Dear Sirs,

Just over a month ago now, I bought a brand new pair of SpikoSpeedoShoes, the new 'running sensation' from your company.

Before I bought them, I was impressed by the fact that they were made using the latest technology and the very best waterproof materials. In addition, I thought the new polypropertine cushioned sole would help my running performance,

For the first two weeks after I bought them I was very pleased with the way they improved my running performance and many times felt like I was 'running on air'.

However, I was very surprised that after two weeks the laces snapped too easily and even more surprised to find that the special sole, which is so important in a running shoe, came apart and let the water in. By the end of the run, my feet were soaking wet! How can I be expected to run well with wet feet?

Considering how much money I paid for them, I do think that the shoes should be much more hard-wearing.

I am returning them straight away to your company, with the guarantee. I would like you to send me either my money back or a new pair of SpikoSpeedoShoes to replace the faulty pair.

I hope that you will reply straight away.

Joanne Cartland

Name _____ Class _____

PCM 21

Terrific tips for a writing workout!

| Tips and suggestions for |

Here are our tips and suggestions to make your writing better still.

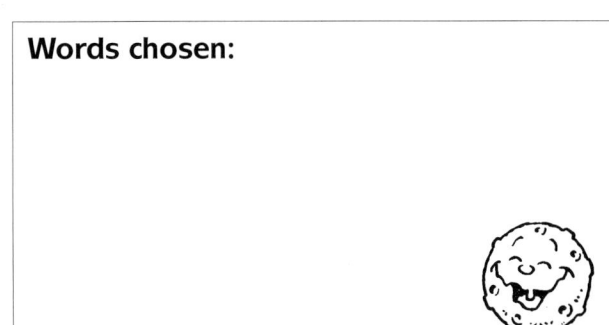

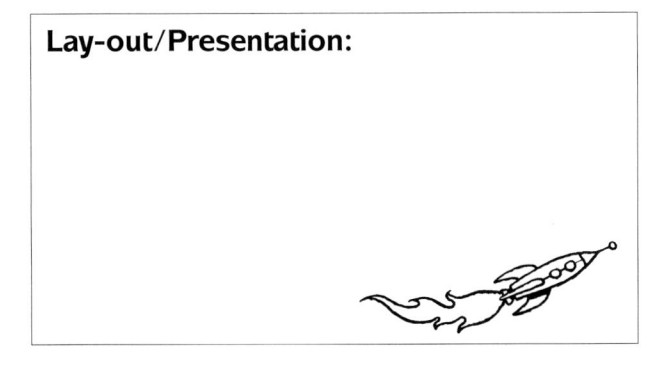

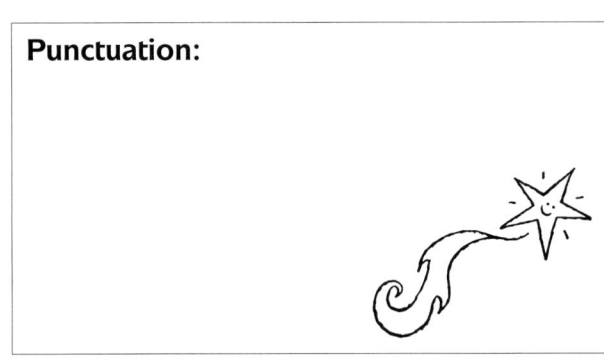

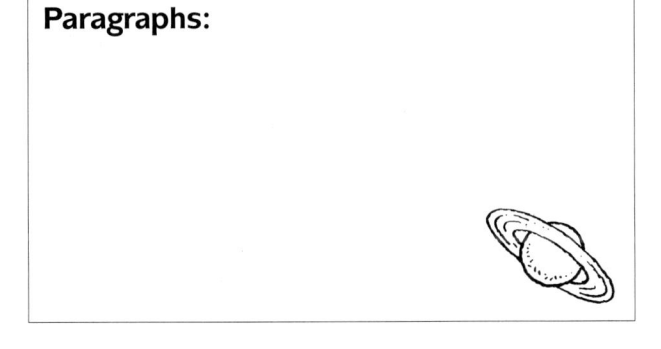

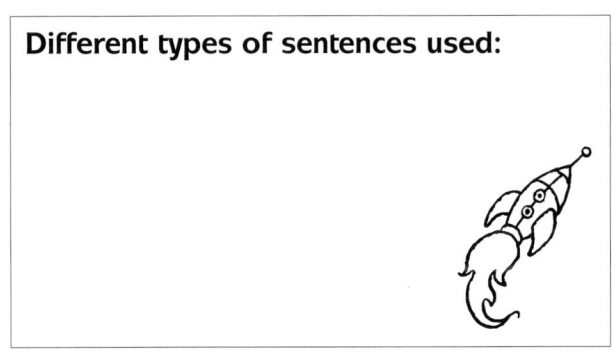

Ideas:

Words chosen:

Lay-out/Presentation:

Punctuation:

Paragraphs:

Different types of sentences used:

Other tips:

Preparing for external tests is, of course, nothing new. In particular, practising different types of writing within set time limits will certainly help your pupils. In this section we consider why preparing our pupils for SATs is valuable, and include some task titles and PCMs to help you in your teaching.

Preparing for SATs

The amount of time you decide to spend preparing for SATs will depend on internal pressures, such things as the ability of your pupils, past results, the attitude of your head teacher, governors and other teaching staff and performance management, and external pressures such as Ofsted, local authorities and parents. You need to strike a balance between two.

Devoting most of the term before the SATs to test practice is too much. That will result in a significant reduction in the time you can spend on other curriculum areas and too narrow a concentration on test requirements for English. On the other hand, too little or no preparation will disadvantage your pupils, and will almost certainly adversely affect your school's overall results.

Using writing tasks from past papers to give pupils some experience of planning and completing writing within 20 minutes (Shorter Task) and 45 minutes (Longer Task) will help your pupils handle the time constraints of the tests and give them greater confidence. It also enables you to remind pupils about features of specific genres and such things as purpose and audience. However, the process of writing does not lend itself to specific test practice; writing skills should have been developed over a much longer period of time. Integrate some of the past test paper writing tasks into units throughout Year 6. In addition, you may want to use some of the test tasks and mark schemes in other year groups as and when they usefully support any units of work.

Remember, you need a balanced approach to test preparation in a subject like English, which is a skills- rather than content-based subject. Good practice, over the whole Key Stage, is ideal.

SATs preparation PCMs

Photocopy Masters 22–24 (see pages 72–74) give teachers and pupils top tips for tackling revision for writing tests and for taking the test paper. Photocopy Masters 25–28 (see pages 75–80) provide fun activities for revising spelling and look at ways to make writing more persuasive.

Overview of writing tasks from past test papers

The list on page 71 gives an overview of the titles, text types, and purpose of writing tasks from past test papers. Use these in other units of work, in cross-curricular writing or for revision purposes. The exemplars and mark schemes attached to each can be particularly helpful to teachers.

Overview of writing tasks from past papers

Persuasive	**Letter**
▶ Time for a change? (Speech to persuade others to a point of view) – 2004 Longer Task (To persuade) ▶ A new toy (Advertisement) – 2003 Shorter Task (To persuade)	▶ A special guest (Invitation to visit school) – 2002 (To persuade) ▶ The amazing creature (Identification request) – 2000 (To describe and inform) ▶ Spider supporter – 1999 (To inform and persuade) ▶ School trip (Letter to parents) – 1998 (To inform and explain)
Descriptive ▶ Eye witness (Account of an accident) – 2004 Shorter Task (To inform) ▶ It's my favourite meal – 2005 Shorter Task (To persuade reader of its appeal) ▶ It's a mystery – 2007 Shorter Task (To describe)	
	Playscript ▶ Scene from a play – 2001 (To entertain) ▶ Can I stay up? – 2005 (To entertain and persuade)
Narrative (To entertain) ▶ The queue (based on a storyboard) – 2003 Longer Task ▶ A change in time (time travel) – 2002 Longer Task ▶ A forgetful character – 2002 Longer Task ▶ A strange tale – 1997 Longer Task ▶ Mystery solved – 2001 Longer Task ▶ Three wishes – 2001 Longer Task ▶ Trapped – 2000 Longer Task ▶ The big event – 2000 Longer Task ▶ Home at last – 1999 Longer Task ▶ If pictures could speak – 1999 Longer Task	**Report** ▶ Tried and tested (Report on a product trial) – 2001 (To inform and explain)
	Diary ▶ Moving away (Two contrasting diary entries) – 2000 (To report/reflect) ▶ Dear Diary (Two contrasting diary entries) – 2006 (To inform and persuade)
	Interview ▶ Read all about it! – 1998 (To inform and develop character)
Information ▶ Community park (Leaflet) – 2002 (To inform and persuade) ▶ Save the grove (Leaflet) – 1997 (To persuade) ▶ Seaworld (Guide) – 1999 (To inform and persuade) ▶ Endangered creature – 2006 (To inform and describe) ▶ Save it! (Leaflet) – 2007 (To explain and persuade)	

PCM 22

SAT-NAV for teachers

- Create a positive climate:
  - Build confidence with positive class, group and individual feedback. Stress progress made rather than errors.
  - Make the marker 'human' by introducing 'Sid and Sybil the SATs markers'; this makes the external marking process less threatening and also means that we can tell pupils what markers are looking for. This will help them when they take the test.
  - Use AfL approaches (see pages 4–10).
  - Give pupils as much choice and independence as possible.

- Analyse both good and not-so-good writing models. Break down mark schemes into 'ladders' to show progression.

- Build in reflection time after writing has been marked. Help pupils to identify learning opportunities and insist that some changes are made to improve work.

- Give careful thought as to whether to tell pupils the levels they achieve in writing. This can be motivating or discouraging, depending on the pupil. It can also encourage complacency. Pupils fluctuate as a result of the stimulus, amount of support, the task and how they feel on any particular day!

- Remember to set aside time for *writing for pleasure*. Writing journals, in which pupils have complete freedom and choice, should be encouraged.

- A persuasive purpose is common to many different text types (see page 49 for some examples of past writing tasks). Revise different ways of writing persuasively (see PCM 28, page 80).

PCM 23

SAT-NAV for Year 6 teachers

Explain to pupils that while they need to write factually and accurately in other areas of the curriculum, in English they are trying to 'show off' their writing skills. They can 'invent' ideas and pretend they are true using such phrases as 'Everyone knows that …', 'Seven out of ten people agree that …', 'At least 80% of children …'.

Encourage pupils to refer frequently to their *Word robbery book* (see page 20) to remind themselves of ambitious vocabulary.

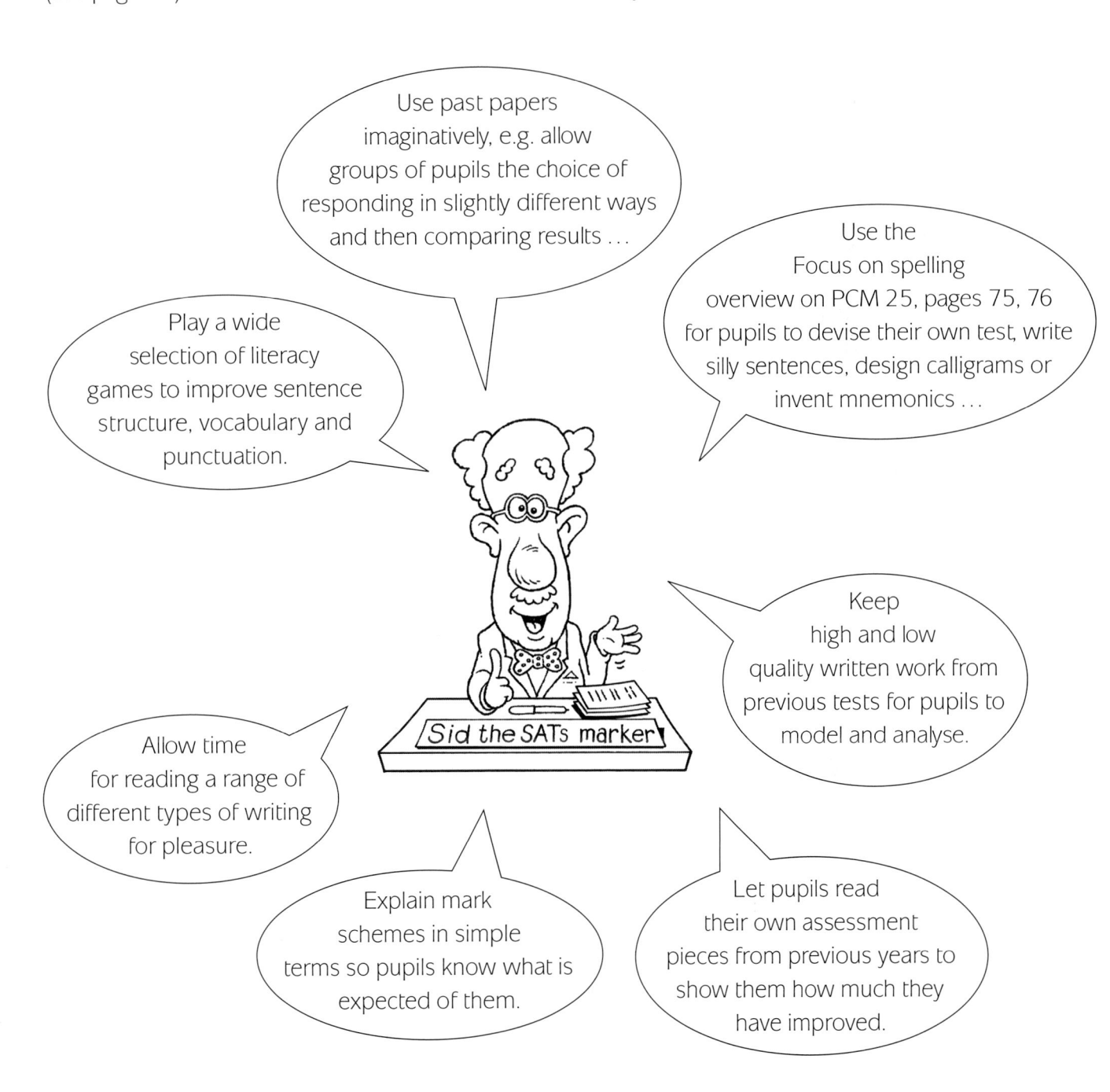

Sid the SATs marker

- Use past papers imaginatively, e.g. allow groups of pupils the choice of responding in slightly different ways and then comparing results …
- Use the Focus on spelling overview on PCM 25, pages 75, 76 for pupils to devise their own test, write silly sentences, design calligrams or invent mnemonics …
- Play a wide selection of literacy games to improve sentence structure, vocabulary and punctuation.
- Keep high and low quality written work from previous tests for pupils to model and analyse.
- Allow time for reading a range of different types of writing for pleasure.
- Explain mark schemes in simple terms so pupils know what is expected of them.
- Let pupils read their own assessment pieces from previous years to show them how much they have improved.

PCM 24

SAT-NAV for writers

Get into gear to find your way round the writing paper!

Before you move off:

- Listen carefully to instructions about the task. Read it for yourself. Try to show that you know **what type** of writing it is, **who** it is being written for and **why** it is being written. Make sure that YOU STICK TO THE TASK SET. Have a check point halfway through your writing when you make sure that your diary or speech, for example, has not become a story.

- Use the planning sheet to your advantage. It is a guide to help you but you can also add your own ideas.

- Do not be afraid to write ideas and phrases outside the planning boxes.

- Do not spend too long on your planning. Plan quickly without worrying about presentation.

- Use any helpful reminders for connectives, vocabulary and punctuation.

During the test:

- Set out to 'WOW' your marker with the best words you can think of.

- Do not think everything you write has to be the truth. You are trying to 'show off' your writing skills.

- Leave enough time to include an ending.

PCM 25a

Focus on spelling

An overview of words set on previous papers grouped according to structure or letter strings.

This list can be used to devise tests for Year 6 pupils and to provide a bank of words for display. Taking one word from four different sections or four words from the same section, pupils can also devise their own tests.

▶ **Short vowel + double consonant**
stopped, follow, million, different, common, trapped, slippery, attempts, swimming, planned, difficult, pollution, sunny, opposite, accuracy, disappeared, supply, approached, corridor
▶ **Silent letters**
wrestling, building, known, knowledge, castles, climbing, environment, carriages, fascinating, whiskers, doubt, bristling
▶ **Adding '-ly' to words ending in '-e'**
approximately, extremely, probably, effectively
▶ **Adding '-ly' to words**
frequently, particularly, perfectly, smoothly, thoroughly, importantly, directly, ravenously
▶ **Adding '-ly' to words already ending in '-l'**
actually, generally, physically, carefully, gradually
▶ **Soft 'c' followed by 'y', 'e' or 'i'**
accuracy, participate, century, cities, centre, practice, produce, process, medicine, recent
▶ **Soft 'g' followed by 'i' or 'e'**
original, emergency, generally, change, passenger, engines, carriages, advantage, rigid
▶ **Adding '-ing' to verbs**
vanishing, swimming, challenging, raising, inspecting, escaping, interesting, including, beginning, moving, extinguishing, causing, expecting, lying
▶ **Past tense of verbs with '-ed'**
involved, delivered, required, developed, camped, arrived, grabbed, surveyed, scattered
▶ **The letter 'y' changing to 'i' + '-es'**
bodies, families, cities, varieties, properties
▶ **The letter 'y' changing to 'i' + '-ed'**
carried, qualified
▶ **Adding 'y' to root words**
noisy

PCM 25b

▶ **The '-ful' suffix** colourful, successful, hopeful	▶ **'ure'** injured, future, ensure, structures, texture
▶ **The '-less' suffix** regardless, effortless	▶ **'-ous' and '-ious'** serious, mysterious, cautiously, enormous, ridiculous
▶ **The vowel digraph '-ea-'** creatures, spreading, released, ready, realistic, rehearsed, gleaming, healthy, disease, release, head	▶ **'qu' and 'gu'** qualified, disguised, headquarters
▶ **The vowel digraph '-ai'** straightened	▶ **'-le'** tumble, capable, available, uncomfortable, sensible
▶ **The vowel digraph '-ee-'** breeze, sneezed, between	▶ **'-ation' and '-tion'** generation, foundations, inspection, invention, direction, destination, attention, additional, distraction
▶ **The vowel digraph '-ou'** proud	
▶ **The vowel digraphs '-ie-' and '-ei-'** believe, weight, pierce, varieties, friends, height	▶ **'exc-'** exciting, excited, excellent
	▶ **The 'al-' prefix** almost
▶ **The vowel digraph '-oi'** voice	▶ **The 'dis-' prefix** disappeared
▶ **The cluster '-dge-'** judged, hedges	▶ **'im-'** important
▶ **The superlative '-est'** largest, nastiest, widest, biggest	▶ **'ough'** enough, roughly, thorough
▶ **The letter string 'ual'** actually, unusual, individual, gradually	▶ **Plurals adding 's'** females, anchors, surroundings
▶ **The letter string 'ial/al'** special, material, essential, natural	▶ **Tricky spellings** journey, countryside, necessary, surprise, advertise, designed, technique, selects, strength, remember, design, physical, surprising, survive, illuminate, vary, intruder
▶ **The 'trans-' prefix** transformed, transported	
▶ **'-lf' changing to '-lves'** themselves	

Name _____ Class _____

PCM 26

Spelling high jump!

Use your knowledge of spellings and a dictionary to see how high you can 'jump' by adding more words to the list. Start on the bottom line in each box and write one word per line until you reach Gold!

'ful' ending (one 'l' only)

colourful   hopeful
successful   careful

'ial' pattern

special   material
essential   initial

'ous' ending

famous   zealous

'less' ending

careless   regardless
effortless   hopeless

'gu' pattern
(five or more letters)

guard   guarantee
disguise   guess

'exc' pattern

excited   excellent

'dge' pattern

judged   hedges
ledge   nudged

'ure' pattern

injured   future
structure   sure

'le' ending

tumble   capable

'ual' pattern

actual   unusual
individual   gradual

'ious' pattern

serious   mysterious
vicious   suspicious

'al' beginning

also   almost

Name _____   Class _____

PCM 27a

Spelling puzzles

Try these puzzles to make spelling test revision more fun!

1 washing Make new words by adding 'ashing' to these beginnings. Tick any which have the same sound as 'washing'. gn_____ sm_____ l_____ cr_____ b_____ c_____	**2 before** How many times does the letter 'e' occur in the word 'before'? Spell 'before' aloud three times.
3 healthy How many three-letter words can you make out of the word 'healthy'? _____ _____ _____	**4 disease 5 release** Same 'ease' but different sound. Write three more words with 'ease'. _____ _____ _____
6 Circle the correct spelling. cerious serious sereous serious serious serius	**7 lairetam** This word is written backwards. What is it? Try to work it out before writing it down. _____
8 process Find this word in the wordsearch. w j g a m e n t p j d e e l m u r t a c s x m t o e f r a z v s c w b e y o v e e x g j a w y u s a s d f c a o s g h e p n a	**9 essential** It is ESSENTIAL that you can spell this word. LOOK, COVER, WRITE and then check your spelling of it. _____

Name _____ Class _____

PCM 27b

10 available This is one of a group of very able spellings. How quickly can you find three 'able' words with more than two syllables? _____able _____able _____able	11 survive I want to text you the word 'survive'. Which numbers on a mobile would you press to spell it?
12 supply Complete these phrases with a word starting with 's'. Socks supply _____ Santas supply _____ Sandwiches supply _____	13 surprising Which letter in this word is often not pronounced and sometimes missed out when we spell it? _____
14 advantage How many three-letter words can you find in 'advantage'? _____ _____ _____	15 properties 16 varieties Underline the ending which is the same in both these words. Which one has more vowels?
17 medicine Draw a bottle of Marvellous Medicine and label it with the word above.	18 physical Underline the opening letters or each word below as far as they are the same as the letters of 'physical'. (Look carefully!) physician psychic physics physicist physique
19 remember Can you remember how many 'm's in this word? ☐	20 design ... contains the word 'sign'. Underline the word 'sign' every time you see it in this sentence: **Please design a sign on this signpost and signify its importance with a signature.**

PCM 28

We have ways of persuading you ... to protect the planet!

Here are six different ways of making your writing more persuasive.

1 Replace 'weak' words with 'strong' ones

very bad → catastrophic

throwing → hurling

harmful → deadly

damaged → destroyed

2 Put questions to the reader

- Do you really want to ... ?
- Will we never learn that we ... ?
- Are you up to it?
- Can't you see that ... ?
- How will the earth survive if we ... ?
- When will we wake up to the fact ... ?
- Isn't it about time that ... ?
- Are you ready and willing to ... ?
- Do you want to play your part?

3 Appeal directly to the reader

YOU can make a difference!

The responsibility is YOURS!

YOU need to act today!

4 Repetition/patterns for effect

Think ... just think about ...

REcycle, REuse and REspect

Every time you place one, just one ...

The MORE you recycle, the LESS you waste.

5 Use facts and figures

If you don't know any facts and figures, you might have to make them up to practice and show off your writing skills. Here are some examples:

Over 90% of the cars on the roads ...

Eight out of ten people do not do enough ...

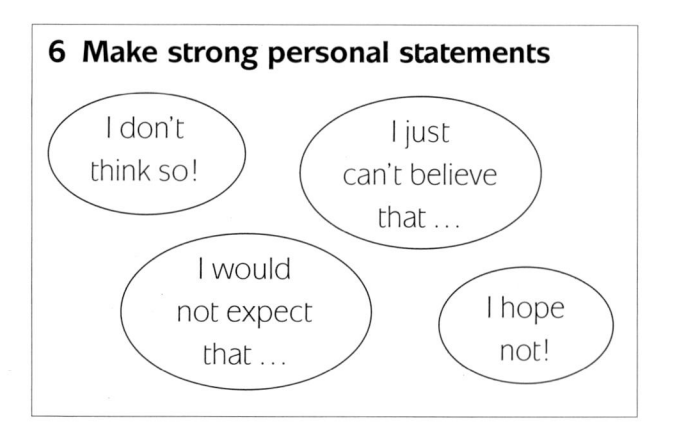

6 Make strong personal statements

- I don't think so!
- I just can't believe that ...
- I would not expect that ...
- I hope not!